LINCOLN CHRISTIAN

P9-CQM-261

PRAISE FOR

THE ULTIMATE SURVIVAL GUIDE FOR CHILDREN'S MINISTRY WORKERS

Ivy and I have worked together, so I know from experience that she is one of the most knowledgeable, skilled and experienced leaders of children's ministry in America. She combines education, experience, expertise and passion to communicate to volunteers everything they need to know about effective children's ministry.

Leith Anderson

Pastor, Wooddale Church, Eden Prairie, MN
President, National Association of Evangelicals, Washington, DC

Ivy combines the mind of an educator with the insight of a ministry veteran and the heart of a shepherd to create a great handbook for anyone engaging in the high calling of ministering to children and the family. Whether you are a new children's ministry worker looking for help in how to work with kids or a seasoned children's pastor looking for great training materials, this book is for you! Ivy has hit a home run with this book and the insight it contains.

Pastor Greg Braly

Family and Children's Ministry Pastor,
Crystal Evangelical Free Church
National Point Person for Family and Children's Ministries,
Evangelical Free Church of America

THE ULTIMATE SURVIVAL GUIDE
FOR
CHILDREN'S MINISTRY WORKERS

Ivy Beckwith

Gospel Light

From Gospel Light
Ventura, California, U.S.A.

Published by Gospel Light
Ventura, California, U.S.A.
Printed in the U.S.A.

© 2007 Ivy Beckwith.
All rights reserved. Published in association with the literary agency
of Alive Communications, Inc., 7680 Goddard Street, Suite 200,
Colorado Springs, Colorado, 80920, www.alivecommunications.com.

Library of Congress Cataloging-in-Publication Data
Beckwith, Ivy, 1954-
  The ultimate survival guide for childrens ministry workers / Ivy Beckwith.
    p. cm.
  ISBN 0-8307-4366-9 (trade paper)
  1. Christian education of children. 2. Church work with children. I. Title.
  BV1475.3.B43 2007
  259'.22—dc22   2006102725

1 2 3 4 5 6 7 8 9 10 / 10 09 08 07

Rights for publishing this book in other languages are contracted by
Gospel Light Worldwide, the international nonprofit ministry of Gospel
Light. Gospel Light Worldwide also provides publishing and technical
assistance to international publishers dedicated to producing Sunday
School and Vacation Bible School curricula and books in the languages
of the world. For additional information, visit www.gospellightworld
wide.org; write to Gospel Light Worldwide, P.O. Box 3875, Ventura,
CA 93006; or send an e-mail to info@gospel lightworldwide.org.

This book is dedicated to all the wonderful children's ministry volunteers I've had the privilege to work with over the years. All of you at Northwest Baptist Church, Grace Chapel, Wooddale Church, Colonial Church and now the Congregational Church of New Canaan —you know who you are.

405

117175

CONTENTS

- How do I find out what my responsibilities are?
- What time should I plan to arrive for class?
- How much outside prep time should I plan for?
- Why is "volunteer training" important?
- What is the key to making a difference in kids' lives?
- How can I be a valuable member of the children's ministry program?
- How can I inspire kids to love the Bible?
- What part do I play in the kids' spiritual growth and understanding?

- What do I need to remember as I prepare for my first day?
- How do I get to know the kids in my group?
- How do I build relationships with my group outside of church?
- How do I ask questions that kids will want to answer?
- How do I lead a discussion with younger children?

The Home Connection

The Red Tape

Children's Ministry Work: A High Calling

Reluctant Volunteers

FOREWORD

I first met Ivy Beckwith at a pastoral "vision and dreaming" retreat 20 years ago. She was the new Minister to Children (fresh in town that weekend) for our very large, high-profile church, and I was a very nervous youth ministry intern attending my first staff retreat. The staff had been asked to share personal ministry dreams and specific goals for the upcoming year. As we went around the circle, the group dynamic became more competitive, each speaker spoke a bit longer than the previous colleague and the professed goals became more and more grandiose. (The vision statements were beginning to fall just an eyelash short of world peace and the evangelization of all known population groups.)

When Ivy's turn came, she offered only a few brief statements with obvious humility and wisdom. She voiced her intention *not* to make her mark by fixing or changing ministry elements that were already working well. Her hope was to spend the majority of her time building relationships with

the paid staff under her supervision and with volunteers, children and families. Her most immediate objective was to ask really good questions. After
those brief statements, I whispered to a friend on
staff, "I really like her: wise, relationally biased and—
heaven forbid—practical."

I still really like Ivy Beckwith, and with good
reason. Her résumé includes directing children and
family ministries in smaller churches and mega-
churches, churches with innovation expectations
and churches with nonnegotiable traditions, urban
churches and suburban churches, churches in a wide
variety of cultural and geographical settings . . .
oh, and development work with several curriculum
publishers. Her experience is vast and varied. I cannot think of a better person to guide volunteers and
professionals through the challenges and opportunities of children's ministry.

I've had the privilege of serving with Ivy on the
Board of Directors at Mars Hill Graduate School in
Seattle, Washington, and on the leadership team of
Emergent Village (emergentvillage.com). These communities provide her with a unique perspective on
the intersections between a postmodern culture
and the practices of ministry. Her experience and
relationships combine to make her truly a singular
voice in the vision for and management of children's ministry.

The meeting point of cultural reality and the mission of the church form the "back story" for much of the practical advice Ivy shares in this book. She understands that we serve in changing cultural contexts of ministry. The demographic and sentimental compositions of what we call "family," the climate of daily life for children (threats, obstacles, technologies and possibilities), and the expectations that participants place on Christian community have all changed dramatically over the last couple of decades. This book allows cultural transition to converse with the most essential practicalities of children's ministry.

I recently transitioned into church planting. We are starting with a blank slate of experience and tradition of children's ministry in our context, and I'm eager to share this resource with others who are crafting and shaping ministries to children. I believe its insights will help your ministry community (and ours!) move far beyond survival mode to an environment of exciting spiritual formation and transformation. In this *Ultimate Survival Guide,* Ivy is still asking and answering great questions, just like that first night on our staff retreat 20 years ago.

Tim Conder
Founding Pastor of Emmaus Way
Durham, North Carolina

INTRODUCTION

Today's church is full of dedicated volunteers working in children's educational programming. They are enthusiastic. They genuinely love being with kids. And they are dedicated to helping children learn to love Jesus.

But I've seen something happen with these eager, committed servants. Because they don't have the basic skills needed for working successfully with children, or because they don't understand this generation of children and how they learn, they get bogged down, frenzied, discouraged and—ultimately—burnt out. My prayer is that this book can give volunteers some simple, practical tools for working with children of all ages, and help them understand the eternal importance of their jobs.

A few years ago, a certain politician endured a lot of ridicule when she quoted the old African proverb "It takes a village to raise a child." She was criticized by some who thought she was downplaying the importance of the nuclear family. While I can't speak to her intentions, I think it's deeply important to acknowledge that God never created the nuclear family to go it alone. The dependence on the nuclear family for a child's welfare is a relatively new occurrence—in Bible times, it was the extended family and the entire tribe that took the responsibility for raising the children. It did, indeed, take a village.

Things are no different today. Hundreds of studies have shown that kids grow to emotional and spiritual health when they have the advantage of positive relationships with many adults, rather than just a few.[1] As a children's ministry volunteer, you now have the opportunity to be one of those people to the kids in your faith community.

Faith doesn't grow in a vacuum. God designed faith to be communal and relational, and kids need a faith community as much as adults do . . . maybe more. Kids need to know there are adults at their church who know them by name, enjoy being with them and think they're special. These healthy, unique relationships with adults go further to help kids learn to love God and follow Jesus than any lesson on the structure of the Tabernacle ever will . . . as fascinating as that might be to some people!

Some people who volunteer to work with kids in children's ministry believe that the best way to help kids learn to love God and follow Jesus is through teaching Bible facts and moral applications of those

Bible facts. Now, there is nothing wrong with Bible facts and good values—I'm a big fan of both!—but I'm not convinced that facts and values fully nurture and care for the souls of children. What kids ultimately need for their healthy spiritual development is time, attention and tender guidance. (Think about how Jesus cultivated relationships with the disciples.) By simply being with the kids at your church—by getting to know them and building relationships with them—you can positively affect their spiritual formation.

In this book, you'll find practical advice and guidelines for volunteering in your church's children's ministry. Practical and hands-on tips are vital—that's why I wrote this handbook, after all!—but I'd like to challenge you not to lose sight of the big picture: helping kids learn to love God and follow Jesus. Whether or not you choose to follow this book's suggestions about how to teach with curriculum or how to keep the attention of preschoolers (and I hope you do), I urge you to do the following:

Be a good model of a person who follows Jesus. This means that you need to love and care about kids, and your love and care need to come through even on days when they drive you crazy. It means that you need to show integrity by upholding the commitment you have made to them and to the volunteer responsibilities you have undertaken. It means that you need to treat kids with courtesy and respect, and set boundaries for them as you help them develop their own self-discipline. It means that you need to share your faith story when you have an opportunity. You can talk with them about times God has comforted you and times when you've not acted as a Christian should. Kids need to see authentic Christian living and will appreciate hearing that sometimes you don't always make the best choices.

Sometimes when I teach workshops for children's ministry volunteers, I ask the participants what they remember about their childhood church experiences. They never remember specific Bible lessons, but they do remember—for good or ill—the people who taught those lessons to them. If you love kids and come prepared each week to be present with them, you're modeling positive characteristics of a person of faith.

Pray for kids and with kids. Put them on your daily prayer list. Think about and pray for each child in your group as you prepare for your volunteer responsibilities. Pray for their families, too. When you are with them—especially if you work with a small group of children—pray with them. Ask them to share their prayer requests with the group, and share the things you'd like them to pray about for you. Even young children can and want to do this for you and each other.

Connect what you're teaching to kids' lives. Help them explore ways they can realistically apply God's story to their own story. Challenge them to try living God's way, and then be sure you talk with them about what happened when you see them next. Kids need to experience what they're learning to make it real in their lives. Encourage them to talk about their life experiences with you, and brainstorm ways to make what you're teaching relevant and meaningful to their lives.

Love kids and live in relational community with them. Kids don't become people who love God and follow Jesus simply by being fed lists of things to believe. Kids become real people of faith when they are in relationships with people who love them in a community of faith. Kids become Christians when they are an integral part of the faith community, doing things for the community as well as having things done for them. Kids develop trusting and authentic relationships with God when they are in trusting and authentic relationships with adults who love both God and kids.

I've designed this book to be helpful to children's ministry volunteers in both large and small churches, working in a variety of settings and in various roles. If you volunteer on a Sunday morning in a traditional role as a teacher or small-group leader, if you lead games during a mid-week program or care for babies in the nursery, you'll find tips and hints in these pages that will help you be successful. If you're a leader of volunteers, I suggest using this resource as part of your training and preparation program.

When I recruit a volunteer into a children's ministry position, my fervent prayer is that the experience be a good one. I do everything I can to enable that volunteer to be fulfilled in this important—but not always easy or rewarding—job. I'm always on the lookout for valuable tools to equip them for success, and my hope is that this book will become one of those tools for you and your ministry.

Never, ever think that you're not having a spiritual impact on the kids you work with at church. Many times, little things that you'd never think would have an impact end up making all the difference, and you don't hear about it until long after the fact. Don't be discouraged by not seeing immediate results—spiritual formation is a lifelong process. It's easy to see kids week after week and never have any idea how their souls are developing. You must trust God to grow the fruit after you've faithfully sown the seed. If you're faithful in the soul care of kids, God will produce the fruit.

Note
1. "Hardwired to Connect: The Scientific Case for Authoritative Communities," The Commission on Children of Risk, 2003.

CHAPTER 1

BEFORE YOU BEGIN

You've agreed to be a children's ministry volunteer. Congratulations! You are embarking on a great adventure. Helping kids learn more about Jesus is one of the most important and rewarding jobs in any church. I'm sure you're excited about impacting young hearts and minds, but I bet you're also a little nervous—especially if you've never done this before.

If you're just the slightest bit anxious, this book is for you. (I hear that sigh of relief!) In it, you'll find the information you need about what to expect and how to prepare for it. Wondering how to pull off an activity with a large group of squirrelly six-year-olds? Looking for some methods to cope with kids who have ADHD? Questioning how best to use Bible curriculum in your fifth-grade small group?

The answers to these questions and much, much more can be found in the following chapters. But let's not get too far ahead of ourselves.

First things first . . .

HOW DO I FIND OUT WHAT MY RESPONSIBILITIES ARE?

I hope that when you were asked to become a children's ministry volunteer, you were given a job description that outlined the responsibilities and expectations of your volunteer position. If you didn't receive one, run—don't walk—to your telephone and call the person who recruited you. Ask to see a job description. If the person responds to you with "What job description?" take a deep breath and ask him or her to explain your job responsibilities. Ask that the explanation be very specific. Take good notes and create your own job description.

If you vaguely remember being given something that looked like a list of job responsibilities, find it and read it thoroughly. If you have questions about any of the responsibilities or expectations, immediately contact the person who recruited you and ask. It's easier to be a great volunteer when you know exactly what is expected of you.

Talk with people who are already working as children's ministry volunteers. These seasoned veterans can offer helpful insights about the ins and outs of the job that you just won't find in a job description. They know the questions to answer before they're even asked, because they remember what it's like to be a new volunteer and they know what you need to know better than anyone else.

Watch the children's ministry program in action to get the inside scoop on the job. If the program is still in session, make plans to observe it in action. You'll see what the kids are like and how the volunteers work with each other and with the elements of the program. You'll see other volunteers doing the job you've volunteered for.

Just remember when you observe an experienced volunteer in action that the person you're watching is just that: an *experienced* volunteer. Sometimes when I recruit people to be children's ministry volunteers, they are reluctant to take on the position because they have seen really excellent volunteers in action—and they're intimidated! They look at how well these people do their jobs and worry they'll never be able to do the same job as well. Remember: Those experienced volunteers were rookies, once upon a time. Use them as great models, but don't expect to immediately be able to do everything they do. Give yourself time! Before you know it, you'll be one of the excellent ones, too.

Now that you know what's expected of you, let's get into the nuts and bolts of planning, preparation and training.

WHAT TIME SHOULD I PLAN TO ARRIVE FOR CLASS?

As you read through the job description, you'll probably find a sentence or two telling you how many minutes early to arrive. Arriving on time means being there before the first kids turn up. (Is that groaning I hear? It's already a challenge to get you and your family out of the house and on time to church—and now I'm telling you to leave even earlier?!)

Arriving before the kids gives you time to get your supplies together and complete the setup so that when the kids show up, you can give all your attention to them—which is the most important thing! You should use every minute possible to focus on the kids, so put everything in order before the first child walks through the door. When she does, be ready to say "hello" and involve her in a Bible-related activity or a conversation about her week.

> # TO PREPARE FOR SUCCESS: PREPARE!

Maybe a story will help convince you that arriving early is not impossible. Not too long ago, I was Children's Pastor at a large church in New England. We had a couple that taught preschoolers during the 9:30 A.M. Sunday School hour and they were always at the church building early. The crazy thing is that they were the parents of five little girls! My assistant and I marveled at how this family could make it to church early when those with no children had trouble making it on time.

Finally one day we asked them how they did it. "Oh, it's easy," the teachers replied. "On Saturday night we do baths and tights. The girls sleep in their tights so that when they wake up on Sunday morning, we can throw on their dresses, comb their hair and go out for breakfast." Being effective and available children's ministry volunteers was a priority, so this couple developed a system that got them to church on time—tights and all! If this family could be on time every Sunday, I am confident that you can do it, too.

HOW MUCH OUTSIDE PREP TIME SHOULD I PLAN FOR?

I'll let you in on a little secret: Kids know when you're flying by the seat of your pants. If you meet the kids unprepared, they will eat you for lunch. When you come prepared, on the other hand, they know you care about them and what you're teaching. Think about it: How would you feel if your pastor came unprepared to teach, if he or she decided to just wing it? My guess is that you'd feel like church was a waste of your time. Kids are no different.

Well-prepared teachers are effective teachers. They can deal with unforeseen circumstances and are not easily thrown off course when the unexpected happens (and it always does). When you make time to do a little outside preparation, you'll be the queen of serene or king of calm to your kids and fellow volunteers, ready to handle whatever arises.

A friend of mine meets a lot of people at Sunday School conferences all around the country, and he tells the story of a teacher who told him she prepares her lesson at the red lights on the way to church on Sunday morning. His response to such a shoddy attempt at lesson preparation is to pray that she runs into many long red lights.

Don't be added to this prayer list. Kids deserve the best you can give! Preparing beforehand—*before the drive to church*—will ensure that your best is what you bring.

> # IF YOU FEEL UNPREPARED, YOU PROBABLY ARE!

The amount of outside preparation time depends on your position. Teachers who have the responsibility for engaging kids in the Bible lesson should plan to prepare at least one to two hours each week. Small-group leaders (we call them "shepherds" in our program) need time to orient themselves to the Bible content of the teaching time—maybe 45 minutes to one hour per week.

Volunteers who lead a large-group activity need to be familiar with how the activity relates to the Bible lesson, know the details of the activity and make sure *in advance* that all required supplies are present and accounted for—about 45 minutes to one hour per week. Finally, if you're one of the super-heroes or heroines in a smaller church who does a combination of all of the above, you should plan for two to three hours per week. But remember, you don't have to do all your prep in one sitting!

Here are a few tips to help you feel better prepared:

- Don't be afraid to ask someone who you think is effective at doing the same job how much time he spends in preparation.

- Think of your prep time as an investment, not a burden.

- Build time into your week—don't wait until the last minute.

WHY IS "VOLUNTEER TRAINING" IMPORTANT?

Training will make you a more effective and confident volunteer. You'll receive ideas for successful teaching, you'll better understand the kids, and your ministry skills will be sharpened.

Sharing the training experience with other children's ministry volunteers will help you understand that many of the challenges you confront are also faced by other volunteers—you'll see that you are not alone! You can learn from the experiences of others, and perhaps you'll even find someone with whom you can talk and share ideas outside of formal volunteer training meetings.

If you find that these meetings are not helpful to you, don't just give up on them. Talk to the person in charge and see if changes can be made that might make them valuable. If you find it impossible to attend training due to scheduling conflicts, ask if there is some training you might be able to do independently through books or DVDs.

WHAT IS THE KEY TO MAKING A DIFFERENCE IN KIDS' LIVES?

Love the kids is the foundation on which your service as a children's ministry volunteer must be built. As you help kids love God and learn to follow Jesus, you'll be most effective by loving and respecting each child who is a part of your group. Here are some suggestions:

First, *be intentional.* Meet the kids and get to know them. Find out who they are, where they come from, what they like to do and what they think is hilarious or boring. Learn what makes each one a unique individual and what he or she has to offer.

Second, *love each kid.* Some kids will be easy to love, but others will need to know that they can trust you before they'll become your friend. Still others will come to class with a huge chip on their shoulders, letting you know they would rather be anywhere but here. Regardless, each child needs to know that you are glad to see them. Don't play favorites.

Third, *accept the kids as they are,* asking God to warm your heart toward each child in your group. When kids see you care for and respect them, they value and respect you.

**BE INTENTIONAL.
LOVE EACH KID.
ACCEPT KIDS AS THEY ARE.**

I once worked with a volunteer who on first glance did not look like the prototype for a stellar children's ministry volunteer. He was a crusty, hard-to-please mailman in his late fifties who taught a group of about 10 fourth-graders. But I found out that looks can be deceiving! I discovered how much respect and admiration his class had for him when I ran across several of them roaming the halls, collecting signatures for a surprise birthday card for him. This was a man who took an interest in the lives of each of these kids, and they loved him for it.

HOW CAN I BE A VALUABLE MEMBER OF THE CHILDREN'S MINISTRY PROGRAM?

Work well with others sounds like a category on an elementary school report card, but it's essential to the success of a children's ministry program. Whether you're working with other volunteers or with a supervisor/director, do unto others as you'd have them do unto you!

If you share teaching responsibilities for a class, get to know your team teacher. Plan your teaching year together and talk through your ideas about discipline, contests and treats. Kids find it confusing when one teacher has a list of 12 classroom rules and the other teacher just likes to hang with the kids. Consider teaching together during the first month. That way, the class will get to know both of you in one orientation time instead of two. Young children, especially, need lots of consistency from their teachers.

Be respectful and courteous. This means being on time, calling and/or making arrangements for a substitute if you are unable to be present, and being considerate of your teammates in front of the children. Let someone know when you use up the last of a popular teaching supply, and alert those who teach near you about an especially noisy or rambunctious teaching activity so that they can plan accordingly.

DO UNTO OTHERS AS YOU'D HAVE THEM DO UNTO YOU!

The person who coordinates your area of volunteer ministry and helps you fulfill your job description might be called a department leader, an age-level coordinator, a program coordinator, a Sunday School superintendent, a children's ministry director, or a children's pastor. If you're having difficulty with some of your responsibilities or with the other volunteers, this is the person you should see for help. They want to know what is happening in your program or class and to hear your suggestions about how to make it better.

HOW CAN I INSPIRE KIDS TO LOVE THE BIBLE?

You have the awesome responsibility and privilege of leading kids into the most important Book ever written: the Bible. When you work with kids in your church, you play a major role in their faith journeys—you introduce them to and help them understand God's message of love for each of them.

Through the Bible, God shows us who He is and how much He loves us. He shows us the path toward love, fulfillment, hope, peace and eternal life. Your actions and words live out the importance of this Book and show how much you value it.

For many years, the youth organization Young Life used the sentence "It's a sin to bore a kid" as its motto. In the end, it is your passion and energy that will capture the attention of your students and allow them to leave the class or event with greater faith and love for God. Make your motto "It's a sin to bore a kid, especially about the Bible!"

WHAT PART DO I PLAY IN THE KIDS' SPIRITUAL GROWTH AND UNDERSTANDING?

As you read this chapter, did you start to wonder if you're really up to this "ministry to children" thing? On your own, maybe not—but don't forget that you have the resources of the God of the universe at your disposal! God *wants* you to be an effective children's ministry volunteer. God *wants* you to succeed. God *wants* to work through you to plant seeds of faith in these young minds and hearts.

And that's the key. *God's* part is to bring spiritual growth and understanding to the kids in your class. *Your* part is to create an environment where that can happen. So . . .

- Be on time.
- Be prepared.

- Be eager to attend training meetings.
- Be loving to all the kids—yes, even those who challenge you!—and be a team player.
- Be positive in your attitude, words and actions.
- Be passionate about the Bible.

Remember: You're not on your own!

CHAPTER 2

YOUR FIRST DAY

It is a truly awesome responsibility to model Christian living and talk about God's Word with kids. As you consider it, you might be feeling a little scared or intimidated as you think about meeting your class or small group of children for the first time. It's only natural. Take a deep breath and read on.

WHAT DO I NEED TO REMEMBER AS I PREPARE FOR MY FIRST DAY?

Preparation will alleviate a lot of your nervousness. Great preparation lets you concentrate on the kids. If you're teaching, study the lesson (find out how to use curriculum in the next chapter), know which student pieces to use, and make sure you have all your supplies. If you're a small-group leader, make sure you know what sorts of activities and discussions you'll be leading kids through. If you're leading a group of kids in an activity, know exactly how the activity works before you get there. Even over-preparing can be a good thing for the first few times you teach.

Think ahead of time about ways to get to know the kids in your group. Your ministry leaders may supply you with questions or activities to help you get acquainted, but it's always good to inject your own personality so that they get to know you as well. Find out if the kids know each other. In large churches especially, they may be from several different school districts and might need time to get to know each other.

> # GREAT PREPARATION LETS YOU CONCENTRATE ON THE KIDS.

Keep in mind that it's new for everyone. The kids may be as nervous about being with you as you are with them. Young children especially may be scared to leave their parents and move into a new situation—remember that their reluctance is not about you; it's just a natural part of a young child's development. Because children don't always have the verbal skills to put words to what they're feeling, they may act out their anxieties through difficult or standoffish behavior. Again, this is not about you but about them dealing with their own fears. In one church where I worked, we had a first-grader who never spoke to anyone at church. She talked at home, so we knew that she didn't have speech or hearing difficulties, but she just didn't want to talk much during our church programs. And we didn't force her. We just let her engage in the activities in her own way. Sometimes you just have to introduce yourself, welcome kids and let them warm up to you in their own time.

Take into account that the first day of any children's ministry program is always a bit chaotic. Parents aren't sure where their children belong, volunteers arrive late and don't know where they are supposed to be, and kids end up in the wrong room or group or aren't happy with the class or group they're in. First days are a circus. Just remain calm. Do the job you were recruited to do, the job you've prepared to do. Try to be helpful to parents, kids and the other people in charge. Be part of the solution, not part of the problem.

Last, expect to enjoy the experience! A positive attitude will go a long way toward a wonderful learning experience for you *and* the kids. Of course, there will be some days that are more fun than others and there will be kids that are harder to love than others. But accentuating the positive about your group will make this a good experience for you and for them.

HOW DO I GET TO KNOW THE KIDS IN MY GROUP?

The most important thing you'll do with kids is build relationships with them, and relationship building starts the very first time you meet them. The first impression you make on kids is as important as any first impression you make on adults. Greet each child with enthusiasm, warmth and friendliness—but remember to keep it real.

Work hard at learning their names. Think about how you feel when someone pronounces your name incorrectly or calls you by someone else's name. Well, kids feel the same way! The other day I heard a woman being interviewed on the radio about growing up as an identical twin. One of the difficulties she cited was people who didn't bother to get to know her and her sister as individuals. With a bit of sarcasm, she told about a Sunday School teacher who, instead of calling them by their names, called them "Twin." I was sad as I thought of that Sunday School teacher's missed opportunity to build a loving relationship with those girls. Make sure your kids have nametags and insist that they wear them, at least until you know their names (and they know each others' names!).

Get to know their lives, their families and their likes and dislikes. I worked with one volunteer who always asked any group of kids the same three questions. She asked them what they had for breakfast, their favorite color and about their pets. Because she always asked the same three questions, she never needed to think about what she was going to ask ahead of time. Be prepared to answer the questions you ask the kids. They are as curious about you— perhaps more!—as you are about them.

My Three Get-Acquainted Questions:

1. How many brothers and sisters do you have?

2. What is your favorite food?

3. What is your favorite school subject?

As kids arrive, engage them in conversation. Ask about their week. If it is near holiday or vacation time, ask them about their plans. If you're curious about their lives, pretty soon they'll be volunteering information about themselves before you can even ask.

Meet the parents. When parents drop their kids off at your church program, take the initiative and introduce yourself. Tell them how pleased you are to have their child in your group. Knowing a child's family can help you know each child a little better.

Plan a prayer time each week, and ask the kids for prayer requests and praises to God. Listening to what they say will help you keep up with what is happening in their lives. Remember to keep track of the requests in order to ask the kids for progress reports!

HOW DO I BUILD RELATIONSHIPS WITH MY GROUP OUTSIDE OF CHURCH?

This is a tough question. These days, most children's ministry volunteers don't have time to spend with kids outside of the church program time. Gone are the days of the kindly Sunday School teacher who takes each child out for a soda or an ice cream sundae. And lots of churches don't encourage that kind of thing anymore because of liability issues.

But there are ways to strengthen relationships with kids outside the boundaries of the church program.

Use the mail. If a child is absent from your group or program, send a card or postcard. (Check with the person in charge of your program—some churches have these cards readily available for their volunteers to use.) Ask for a list of birthdays and send birthday cards. They love to get mail.

If your kids have e-mail addresses, send them an e-mail every once in a while. You can even use e-mail to give them a preview of what activities they'll be doing the next time you meet with them. If you choose to do this, let parents know. You don't want your message to get caught in a spam filter or worry parents because their child received an unexpected e-mail from an adult.

Many times the church kids will be in the same sports programs or after-school programs as your own kids, which makes it convenient to see kids outside of the church building. If you do see the kids in your church program, make sure you say "hello" and ask how they're doing.

Of course, the best way to get to know your group outside of the church program is to *do things with them* outside of the church program. If you want to invite your group on an outing or attend their sporting activities, talk first with the supervisor/director in charge of your program. Many churches have guidelines for volunteers for outside activities. These are for your protection, the protection of the children and the protection of the church's resources. If you get the "OK" from the children's ministry leader, make sure the parents know you and approve of the activity you're proposing. Always make sure there are at least two adults present at any outside activity—never, *ever* allow yourself to be alone with one of the kids in your group.

HOW DO I ASK QUESTIONS THAT KIDS WILL WANT TO ANSWER?

One of the best ways to engage children in a Bible discussion is to capture their imaginations with great questions—questions that are age-appropriate and intriguing. But how do you know what makes a great question?

Go first to your curriculum resources—more about curriculum in the next chapter—and review the questions provided for you. Think about the kids in your group and how they might respond to these questions, but remember the curriculum writers don't know *your* kids. There might be better questions to ask than those written in the resources, but they are a good place to start and might spark some ideas for your own questions.

Spend some time remembering the good discussions you've already had with your group. What kinds of questions sparked their interest? Think about the best conversations you've had and ask questions similar to what you asked before.

Think about the Bible story or the topic. What questions do *you* have about it? What kinds of discussion questions would spark your interest to respond? Odds are that your group has the same kinds of questions and interests, especially if your group is older kids.

> # ASKING GOOD QUESTIONS IS AN ART *AND* A LEARNED SKILL.

Ask your group what questions *they* have about the Bible story or topic. I've done this with elementary school-age kids and find that they have lots of great questions. If you don't know the answer to a question they ask, don't be afraid to tell them that you don't know—maybe it could be a group project to research the answer, or you can tell them that you'll let them know the next time you see them. (But make sure you do it!)

Make sure you have your questions written down or you may forget a great question because of distractions, but go over your questions ahead of time so that you're not tied to your teacher's guide or curriculum resource. You don't want to hinder a spontaneous discussion by having your head buried in a book!

Be ready to ask follow-up questions. Kids don't always know how to respond to each other in a discussion and may respond in only one or two sentences (or words!). If you think a child might have more to say on the subject, ask her a question about her answer or ask the other kids to respond to what the first child said.

Asking good questions is an art *and* a learned skill. Think back to classes you've been in when great discussion happened. That discussion probably evolved because the group leader asked thoughtful questions about the topic that inspired the imaginations and critical thinking skills of the group. Good discussions with your group of children will happen when you think carefully about the kinds of questions that will intrigue them and connect with things that are already happening in their lives. Pay attention to the questions suggested in your curriculum, but don't be afraid to develop your own discussion questions that will meet the kids exactly where they are.

HOW DO I LEAD A DISCUSSION WITH YOUNGER CHILDREN?

Older children are more able to answer complex and abstract questions than younger children. With younger children, it's important to ask concrete and factual questions, since they have little ability to take the perspective of others and respond to what other children in the group have said. A question-and-answer session is possible with young children, but a real discussion probably won't work, especially with a group.

Ask younger children factual questions about the story. This helps them to recall the story and to develop sequential thinking skills as they put the pieces of the story in order. If you use a teaching picture as you tell the Bible story, you can point to different items or people in the picture and ask them to tell you who or what that is. If you are playing with a young child, think of ways you can relate the play to the Bible story.

You can invite younger children to "wonder" about the story, which employs their imaginations. Ask them to wonder "why" God asked a certain Bible character to do the particular action in the story. Or ask them to "wonder" about the outcome of a Bible story or a character's actions. Young children can talk richly about Bible stories even without the critical thinking skills of older children.

CHAPTER 3

THE SCOOP ON CURRICULUM

Most churches use published curriculum because it makes life easier for their children's ministry volunteers. The topics and progression of the lessons are planned, the learning activities are defined and designed to be age appropriate, and teaching resources such as colorful pictures, learning games and student pieces are provided for each lesson to engage children in their Bible learning.

WHAT IS CURRICULUM?

A published curriculum is one that is written, edited and printed by either an independent curriculum publisher or a denominational publishing house. Usually these learning materials are provided to the church on a quarterly basis. The Bible is taught through a "scope and sequence" that predetermines what age level will learn what Bible stories when. There are published curricula for Sunday School, children's church, summer day camps and Vacation Bible School, mid-week events and many other types of children's ministry programming.

Usually this curriculum includes a *teacher/leader guide*, which is the main resource for the teacher or lead volunteer. It contains all the lessons for the quarter, with suggestions for learning activities and using the other resources included in the curriculum package. The guide may also include teacher training tips and devotionals. Often there will also be a *teacher resource pack,* which contains all the pictures, games and activities suggested in the teacher/leader guide—or at least instructions for how to make your own! There is usually a set of *student resources*, which are learning tools for the kids to use during the teaching time to reinforce the lesson. You might also receive *student take-home pages* (designed to connect the lesson with the child's home) and/or a *CD of music* that supports the lesson themes.

Many churches use published curriculum because they don't have the time and talent needed to write a solid curriculum for all ages from scratch. Publishing companies employ professional writers who have an understanding of children and education to develop the different pieces of the curriculum—most churches just don't have an army of writers tucked under a rock somewhere!

> # CURRICULUM IS DESIGNED TO MAKE YOUR JOB EASIER AND TO MAXIMIZE YOUR EFFECTIVENESS WITH YOUR KIDS.

All that said, few churches use published curriculum exactly as it is written. Many churches adapt curriculum to fit their children's ministry's particular goals and objectives by adding or subtracting parts of the lessons and activities. Sometimes churches adapt the curriculum to fit a specific kind of program or format model. As you learn the format of your church's program, you'll come to understand how your church uses its chosen published curriculum.

How you, as a volunteer, are expected to use the curriculum depends on what your position is. If you are the only teacher responsible for the class's entire program time, you likely will utilize all the pieces of curriculum that you're given. If you are a small-group leader, you may only be responsible for leading one activity or guiding your kids in a discussion of the Bible story using the student pages. If you work as a storyteller, you'll only need to learn the story and become familiar with the visual resources that go along with it. Your supervisor/director can tell you which pieces of the curriculum are most important for you and instruct you on how to use them.

If your church does use a published curriculum, it's important that you use it. Your children's ministry leaders have carefully selected that particular curriculum because they believe it will help accomplish goals they've established for the children's ministry. If you just do your own thing, you may end up working against your church's goals for the program. Curriculum is designed to make your job easier and to maximize your effectiveness with your kids.

I'M THE ONLY TEACHER IN MY CLASS. HOW DO I USE THIS CURRICULUM?

Wow! You've taken on a big job: leading the class through all the activities in a lesson. Preparation is the key to a rewarding experience for both you and the kids—get comfortable with the curriculum and it will feel like an old friend. Here's what you might receive:

- *Teacher's guide.* In the teacher's guide, you'll find Bible lessons for each week with suggestions for how to best teach a particular Bible story for your age group of children. The teacher's guide is to be just that: a guide. Please don't ever teach directly from the teachers guide. Good preparation before class will help you focus on your class and their questions.

- *Teacher resource pack.* In the teacher resource pack, you'll find pictures that illustrate each Bible story and other resources (such as games and activities) that supplement each lesson. If you didn't receive a resource pack and your teacher's guide refers to it, talk to your supervisor/director to see if it's possible to have one provided.

- *Student activity pages.* Student activity pages are used during each lesson by your class to work through the Bible story and apply it to their lives. The teacher's guide will tell you when and how to use these colorful pages with the kids in your class.

- *Take-home papers.* Take-home papers are given to the kids at the end of class. Their purpose is to help the kids continue to think about the lesson during the week and to help parents know and reinforce the Bible lessons their children are learning at church.

Your teacher training will help orient you to the specific pieces of the curriculum your church uses. If you feel you need more help in understanding how to use the curriculum with your assigned class, go to your supervisor, team teacher or a more experienced teacher to get help. The curriculum pieces are provided to enhance your experience as well of that of the kids in your class.

I'M A LARGE-GROUP ACTIVITY LEADER.
HOW DO I USE THIS CURRICULUM?

Being an activity leader with a big group of kids can be a blast. You get to hang out with kids, lead activities in your interest and talent areas, and every week it's always a little different. Your job may be to tell Bible stories, lead games, or involve kids in art projects, dramas, cooking or service projects. As you lead the large group, you'll have lots of help and support from the teachers and/or small-group leaders (or "shepherds") who have hands-on responsibility for the kids.

As a large-group activity leader, you'll receive a guide for the activities you're expected to lead. It may be a published handbook or in a notebook put together by your church's children's ministry. This guide will detail the specific activity, describe any supplies you might need and explain how it relates to the overall concept being taught.

It's easy to just plunge into the activity and forget that all the parts of the lesson need to be connected if kids are to get the full meaning of the message. If you neglect to make this connection, your activity ceases to be the learning tool it was intended to be. But if you do make the connection—learning happens!

Here's an example: Last month in our first-through-fourth-grade worship time, we experienced

All the parts of the lesson need to be connected if kids are to get the full meaning of the message.

worshiping God through the Lord's Supper. When the kids returned to their classrooms after Chapel, they continued their understanding of this important event in church life by making beautiful communion plates. The teachers were given information about the celebration of the Lord's Supper and its meaning so that they could connect the activity to the chapel service. If they had been unable to do that, the kids would have done a fun craft project—but that's all it would have been. Instead, we created meaning and reinforced the overall message through the project.

I'M A SMALL-GROUP LEADER/SHEPHERD. HOW DO I USE THIS CURRICULUM?

If you've been asked to serve as a small-group leader/shepherd, it probably means that your church's children's ministry program utilizes a Large Group/Small Group Model. This format pulls kids together in a large group (sometimes age-specific, sometimes multi-age) for some learning activities such as games, Bible stories or art projects. Other activities, such as discussion or response to the Bible story, happen in a smaller group with a leader or shepherd.

Your responsibility as a small-group leader is to care for a small group of children. Other responsibilities may include encouraging kids to participate in the large-group activities, leading shorter activities or discussions and helping with general group management duties. The kids in your group may all be in the same grade or the group might be a mix of ages—the size of your church usually determines the mix of the group.

The curriculum resources you receive will usually be in the form of weekly questions designed to help you lead a discussion about the Bible story or topic. (Occasionally, there may be a short activity suggested to supplement the discussion.) Here are some tips about how to engage all the kids in the conversation you lead:

1. Remember that your top priority as a small-group leader is to build relationships with the kids in your group—get to know them and what is going on in their lives and families.

2. Reflect on who the kids are and the ways the story/topic might intersect with their lives.

3. Brainstorm interesting ways to engage the kids, like asking open-ended questions rather than questions with only one correct answer.

HOW DO I PREPARE FOR SMALL-GROUP TIME?

First, *get to know the kids in your small group*. Learn their names. Learn about what they like to do and learn about their families. Knowing these kids well helps you direct the discussions toward ideas and concepts that connect with their particular circumstances.

Second, *know the Bible story and its application*. Even though you may not be responsible for teaching the lesson, always read the Bible story before leading a discussion.

Third, *review the discussion questions* regarding the lesson or Bible story. Think about how your group might respond to those questions. Think about how you would respond to them. And think of some extra questions to throw out to your small group in case you have need of them.

Finally, *be fully engaged* with the kids and active in all the learning centers. Don't sit back and watch—get your hands and your heart in there!

HOW DO I PREPARE TO LEAD A SMALL-GROUP ACTIVITY CENTER?

First, be sure you understand the activity you're leading, and know how it relates to the Bible concept the kids are learning.

If you are the craft or art project center leader, make a model of the project ahead of time so that the kids can see what it might look like. Hint: This also helps you see if the directions are adequate. Give yourself enough time to gather all the supplies you need (with a bit extra just in case).

If you are leading a game, go over the rules thoroughly, making sure you understand how to play the game, and gather all needed materials. Be prepared to answer "what if" questions about the rules. Think in advance about how the game or the building/room space you've been given might need to be adapted in order for the activity to work.

Be enthusiastic when introducing and leading the activity! Even kids reluctant to participate will catch your enthusiasm.

CHAPTER 4

LEARNING STYLES AND AGE-APPROPRIATE TEACHING

It's hard to say what kinds of generational characteristics today's kids will evidence as they grow into adulthood. But social scientists are speculating that:

Technology and technological advancement will continue to be huge in the lives of children—even more so than the generation preceding them. This generation will continue to be in love with technology.

They might have difficulty relating to other people. Recently I was listening to a radio report about psychologists' concerns that kids who grow up in homes where everyone has his or her own room, bathroom and/or workspace are losing the part of family life that is all about being socialized to live with other people. Brothers and sisters may even have their own playrooms, so they're never in situations where they learn about sharing or accommodating another person.

This will be the first North American generation to grow up during the War on Terror. While other generations have dealt with acts of terrorism, this will be the first generation to have the threat of terrorism talked about every day on the news and in their schools, homes and towns. Consequently, trust and safety might be a much bigger issue for these kids than for the preceding generation.

We will only see these generational characteristics come into focus as children reach adolescence and young adulthood—until then, we can only guess. What we *can* know now is how children perceive the world and process information at various ages, and adapt our teaching and communication styles to meet them where they are. We can also be aware that different kids have different learning styles, and tailor our teaching approaches to include each and every child.

HOW DO TODAY'S KIDS LEARN BEST?

Kids learn best when they're in an emotionally and physically safe environment. To create this kind of space, kids need boundaries. They need to know what's expected of them, what they're allowed to do, that the boundaries will be consistently enforced, and that those doing the enforcing will be predictable. Even when they push against them—especially older kids—they want boundaries, because they help kids feel physically and emotionally safe.

Sometimes church volunteers are reluctant to impose boundaries because they want kids to enjoy their church experience. These volunteers think, mistakenly, that kids will only enjoy the church experience if they are allowed to do whatever they want and are allowed to run the show. Other times, volunteers have never been told how to impose and enforce significant boundaries for kids: Be positive, be clear and be consistent. You might need to remind the kids every time you see them about these boundaries. That's okay. But *always enforce them*. Never let the actions of a few kids spoil the church experience for the rest of the class.

KIDS NEED BOUNDARIES.

Kids learn best when their activities are age appropriate. Kids will be frustrated if you ask them to do an activity their bodies and brains can't do yet. Don't ask a three-year-old to cut out intricate patterns and don't ask a first-grader to write a long paragraph. If you are using a curriculum, you can trust that most of the activities will be age appropriate—but you know your kids and the curriculum writers don't, so always gauge an activity by what you know your group of kids can do.

Kids learn best when they are doing, when they have all of their senses involved in their learning. Very few kids learn best by being talked at or read to. Always make sure your kids are actively involved in whatever the learning aims are. As you get to know your group, you'll discover what kinds of activities and discussion questions capture their imaginations and which do not. Plan to use more of what works as you teach your particular age group.

Kids learn best when they know the adults enjoy being with them and care about them. If you look forward to being with your group each time you meet with them, they'll catch your enthusiasm and respond to it. Today's kids are intuitive, and they'll pick up on your body language and attitudes easily. If you don't want to be with these kids, that attitude will show through to them. Be warm, loving and respectful, and gradually they'll be the same way with you.

Kids learn best when they are learning in the ways they learn best, when the learning activity is part of their personal learning style.

WHAT ARE THE THREE LEARNING STYLES AND HOW CAN I TEACH USING ALL OF THEM?

Every person has a preferred learning style. This is the way he learns best. A person can learn outside of his preferred learning style but it's easier to learn when he's involved in activities that favor that certain style. I hope this overview will help you understand the kids in your group better.

1. *Auditory:* The person with this learning style learns best through listening and talking. These are the kids in your group who have the hardest time being quiet—

they always want to answer the question or make a comment. If you give them directions to read for a project, they will still ask you to explain it to them out loud. They respond well to music, discussion and other small-group activities where the kids have the opportunity to talk and listen to each other.

2. *Visual*: These kids learn best through seeing and watching. These are the kids who love to watch a video clip every week. When you show a visual, they have intense interest in it and notice details and colors. These may be the colorful artists in your group as they like to create their own visuals for others to look at. They learn by watching you do something, and often have high reading comprehension when asked to read on their own.

3. *Kinesthetic*: These are the kids in your group who are always moving, constantly fidgeting or doodling on a piece of paper while other people are talking. This can be annoying to a children's ministry volunteer because often we think that they're not listening or paying attention. But that's

not the case—these are the kids who learn by doing. They don't want to hear or see what life was like in Bible times; they want to make the bricks or wear the clothes or build the model of the Tabernacle.

What this all means is that you've got to vary your activities so that you're hitting all the preferred learning styles of the kids in your class. For example, if your volunteer job is to lead a group discussion and you notice that the visual and kinesthetic kids have no interest, then it's time to spice "the discussion" up a bit! Throw in some pictures—or ask the kids to draw pictures about what you're discussing. Alternately, turn the discussion questions into a game where they move around a little bit so that you'll capture the attention of those kinesthetic learners.

It's easy to get stuck in a rut of doing activities that cater to our own preferred learning style, because that's what we're most comfortable with. But we need to remember that kids learn in all sorts of ways, and we need to meet these kids where their learning styles are.

And now some tips for teaching specific age groups . . .

HOW DO I TEACH IN THE NURSERY?

First, notice I said "teach" in the nursery. Many people who work with young children at church see themselves

THE THREE
LEARNING STYLES:
1. AUDITORY
2. VISUAL
3. KINESTHETIC

only as babysitters and fail to realize they have an opportunity to affect the spiritual formation of these children.

That's because infants and toddlers are learning all the time—even when they don't seem to be doing much of anything besides eating, crying and sleeping! Babies learn as a natural part of living, so teaching is accomplished by your every look, word and act. The sounds, words, actions and—most of all—the feelings that are created in the nursery environment build a young child's understanding of God and Jesus and the loving comfort found in the people around her at church. This foundation of love, safety and trust is the beginning of spiritual formation.

For both babies and toddlers, the best teaching session is one in which children play freely in a safe and interesting environment. You can interact with them in a variety of activities, such as singing, playing with toys, reading a book, telling a simple story and caring for their physical needs.

Infants are very sensitive to subtle cues about your attitude, whether positive or negative. What is your posture toward the one kid who always seems to throw up on you when you pick him up? Do you tense as you pick up the child, steeling yourself against the inevitable? He can tell! Conversely, when your words, looks and actions are relaxed and gentle, loving and kind, you teach the baby that people at church can be trusted—and you're building a foundation for that little guy's trust in God.

For toddlers, the best kind of teaching is one on one, so don't expect that young children will sit in a circle and have "group time" . . . or even remain interested in what you're doing for very long! But as you sit on the floor, talking, playing and singing with one or two or three children, focus your conversation and activities in ways that familiarize a child with God's name and His love. If you use a published curriculum, your teacher's guide will have weekly suggestions for focused play that can acquaint young children with Bible themes.

HOW DO PRESCHOOLERS THINK AND LEARN?

Very differently than older children and adults! That's why some volunteers find it difficult to work with preschoolers—they seem like outer-space aliens. It's hard to remember what it was like to think like a preschooler, so here are a few reminders, along with some tips for making a connection with their wonderful, wacky minds.

Preschoolers are making sense out of the world, which means that they sometimes put ideas together in illogical ways. Once when I was the assistant teacher for a preschool class, one of the girls was figuring out the difference between me and the woman who was "the teacher." One day she studied us and listened as "the teacher" described to me the problems with having one's earlobes pierced twice. The young girl looked at both of us and announced, "Miss Ivy has one hole in each of her ears and Miss Marla has two holes in each of hers. That must be because she's the teacher." That was her way of making sense out of her world, which seems cute and illogical to us but to her explained something she was having trouble understanding.

For the most part, let kids figure things out for themselves. It may be tempting to correct them every time they come up with a seemingly random connection, but allowing their minds and imaginations to stretch is an important stage in their development. If you *do* need to correct a child's illogical idea (e.g., "Jesus is my mom!"), make the correction fun and silly, not shameful.

> # FOR THE MOST PART,
> # LET PRESCHOOLERS FIGURE THINGS
> # OUT FOR THEMSELVES.

Preschoolers have little sense of time. Little good comes from telling a sad two-year-old that Mommy will be back to pick him up in one-half hour. It's better to say, "When we're finished with snack it will be time for your mom to come back." This gives the child a concrete idea of when Mom will be back. Young children also can have short attention spans, and you need to keep things moving to keep them interested. The converse is that once they get engaged in a project, it can be hard to pull them away. Young children can be very focused when they're engaged in an activity that has captured their imagination, so have enough activities prepared to keep them busy—but realize you might not need to use them all.

Preschoolers think in terms of concrete actions and ideas, so when you teach them about an abstract concept like love or joy, tie it to a concrete action. You might say, "Jared, when you give your mom the card you made today, you are showing love to her." Then Jared will know that one of the ways we show love to other people is by giving them special cards. When managing preschoolers' behavior, it's best to define desired behavior in positive terms. Rather than saying, "Carolyn, stop running," it's better to say, "Carolyn, we walk when we're indoors."

It's vital to set boundaries for young children. For example, if you don't want them to play with the blocks, say, "We're not playing with the blocks right now, but you can sit at the table and play with clay or color a picture. Those are our choices. Which would you like to do?" Reward positive behavior rather than pointing out the negative behavior. Say, "I'm pleased that Austin is ready for snack." Also, don't expect very young children to be able to share. If a dispute arises over a toy, try to distract the children with another activity or toy.

The more you work with young children, the more you'll understand the way they understand their world. If you use a published curriculum, you can be sure the writers have made the activities age appropriate for a preschooler, but if you have more questions about what these young children can do and understand, meet with your supervisor/director or a more experienced teacher.

HOW DO GRADE-SCHOOLERS THINK AND LEARN?

It's great that you're concerned about how your grade-schoolers learn—you're on your way to being a great children's ministry volunteer!

Grade-schoolers are active and curious. Always involve grade-school kids in "doing" to enhance their learning—never just talk or lecture at them. They love to work on projects, play games, be involved in discussions, and act out dramas. They like to experience what they are learning about. The more time your class or group spends "doing" rather than "listening" the better they will learn what is being taught.

Grade-schoolers like to work together, so allow them to work together on projects. They do this in school, and it helps them to get to know other kids in the small group or class. Make sure that you give the group appropriate behavioral boundaries and expectations for working together, and make sure you enforce them. Kids will inevitably push the boundaries, but it will be a better learning experience for all if you push back. No child will learn if a couple of kids are allowed to control the class through inappropriate behavior.

Finally, *grade-schoolers are still learning how to learn,* and it's very important for them to feel successful in what they're doing. Keep in mind what they're learning in school, and don't ask them to do more than they've mastered there.

> # REMEMBER THAT GRADE-SCHOOLERS ARE STILL LEARNING HOW TO LEARN.

For example, first-graders are just learning to read and write, so ask them to draw pictures rather than write words. If you work with older children, don't involve them in activities they think are for younger children—they will rebel at this even if it's a really great activity. Know your kids and what they can and can't do.

Above all, treat the kids with love and respect. If they know you are excited to be there with them, they'll be excited about learning what you have to teach.

HOW DO TWEENS THINK AND LEARN?

Fifth- and sixth-graders are a lot of fun, but they can be a challenge to people who work with them in children's ministry. They have lots and lots of energy and don't always have the inner resources to control it, so they have to constantly be reminded about appropriate behavior in a variety of situations.

Tweens are "in-between." They're called "tweens" because—while not yet teenagers—they're on the cusp of adolescence. They may look and dress like teenagers, but emotionally they are still children. Some days these kids are playing with their favorite toys and other days they worry about clothes and hair styles . . . and you never know which child is going to show up! I've found that the best programs for fifth- and sixth-graders are those that have the feel of a youth group but include kid-like activities that they still enjoy. (For example, they still like to make crafts as long as the projects are challenging and "cool" enough.)

Tweens are figuring out right and wrong and shades of gray. Emotionally and spiritually, older grade-school-age children are beginning to understand that the world they live in is not completely good or bad—

they are aware of the gray areas in life. They see that good doesn't always get rewarded and bad doesn't always get punished, and this new knowledge of the world bothers them greatly. They strive to maintain fairness in their own lives, and that's why when you play a game with preadolescents, they are picky about every detail of the rules. Their new worldview causes them to question what they've known about God all their lives—they will have lots of questions for you about God and the world. The best thing you can do for them is to take their questions seriously and not be anxious. Try to answer thoughtfully, and if you don't know the answer—or you're not sure there *is* an answer—be willing to admit it. They will respect you for that.

Tweens can think critically about actions and consequences and are better able to think through different life scenarios than younger children. This ability can make them argumentative because they can spar with you about possible outcomes to certain situations. Often they're not doing this to bug you— they're just practicing their new skills! If you can harness this new reasoning ability, it can be a powerful way to help them make their faith real with actions in their lives.

Tweens can be worriers. They are confronted with current events and world problems every day, and they may be concerned about how outcomes might affect them and their family. Situations in their families can cause them worry, too. Marital discord, illness or job loss will cause these kids more concern than younger children because they can foresee the logical consequences of a situation.

As you hear these concerns from your kids, remember to speak God into their lives. Speak to them of God's love, care and concern for them. Let them know that while they may encounter difficult things in their lives and in the world, God and their community of faith will be with them and watch over them. If it is appropriate, share experiences from your life where God has cared for you in difficult circumstances.

> # SPEAK TO TWEENS OF GOD'S LOVE, CARE AND CONCERN FOR THEM.

Tweens need to see examples of Christian faith in action. They need models of people striving to love God and follow Jesus, so introduce them to people who are great examples of what people of faith look like. Remember that preadolescents can smell hypocrisy easily. They need consistent adult models of authentic faith in order for their faith to grow.

Tweens love service projects. They are very tuned in to helping others and making the world a better place. Find meaningful service activities and you'll engage them on another level of learning.

You'll enjoy working with this age group. It's one of my favorites. They're not easy, but they are worth every minute of extra time and preparation.

WHAT DO I NEED TO KNOW ABOUT TECHNOLOGY?

I think the greatest dividing issue between this generation of kids and earlier generations is the technology factor. These kids don't know life without computers, cell phones, the Internet and all the other kinds of hardware and software that proliferate today. Their knowledge about and desire for all these technological gadgets can be disconcerting for those of us who remember when there were only five or six TV channels and who have digital clocks all over the house blinking "12:00." If this is you, here is a brief overview of some technologies that are important to the kids you'll be working with.

The Internet gives kids unlimited access to ideas and people they never would have had access to a few years ago. While I believe most parents try to be vigilant about what their kids do on the Internet, I think most older kids do more online than their parents approve of—and I think we're naïve if we don't think this is true of some younger kids as well. Unless kids discuss what they read online with parents or other trusted adults, they have no way of knowing what's true and real and what isn't. Talk to the kids you work with about the websites they visit and the websites popular with their friends. Visit those websites so that you learn the kinds of things they are interested in.

If you have Internet access at your church, you can use it as a teaching tool. Have your kids look up information on life in Bible times or articles or pictures on a topic you're discussing. You can even find interactive Bible games on the Internet that your group might enjoy playing. At the very least, familiarize yourself with the Web so that you can have intelligent conversations about it with your kids.

Increasingly, instant messaging and text messaging are the ways today's kids stay in touch with each other. Instant messaging (or IMing) is done on the computer. Kids type messages to each other or a group in real time while doing other things online. (These kids think they are the best multi-taskers ever and they attempt to do many things at once!) Even more than IMing, text messaging (or txt) is becoming the communication method of choice. This is done from a cell phone. When the key pad is memorized, messages can be sent quickly and quietly—even during church programs or worship services—and real-time conversations can be had. Be aware that kids these days are not in need of face-to-face or phone contact in order to build and maintain peer relationships, which can make it harder for parents to maintain control and access to their children's friends.

> **ANYONE WHO WORKS WITH KIDS NEEDS TO UNDERSTAND HOW TECHNOLOGY IS SHAPING THE KIDS OF TODAY.**

Kids love iPods (and other mp3 players) and every one wants one. These little gizmos allow you to download music, video and other kinds of electronic media (such as podcasts) from the Internet and then listen to them at your leisure. The iPod can store thousands of hours of entertainment, and many kids today walk around all the time with earphones in their ears (while texting their friends). Even if you don't ever plan to own one of these gadgets, it's important for you to know what they are. The kids you work with will be talking about them, and they'll be more likely to listen to you if they think you understand something about their world.

With technology, the biggest concern is not so much that we're as savvy as the kids, but that we know something about how it's changing the way they look at and understand the world around them. Technology has changed the way they think and the way they expect to be taught, and the way they expect to investigate concepts and ideas. Anyone who works with kids in the church setting needs to be aware of these changes and understand how technology is shaping the kids of today.

CHAPTER 5

MANAGING THE CHAOS

Learning styles and age-appropriate teaching are well and good as long as your group of kids is well behaved—so how do you make sure they are? In this chapter, we'll look at how to head off behavioral problems before they occur, and how to deal with them when they happen.

HOW DO I GET AND KEEP THE KIDS' ATTENTION?

It's incredibly important to engage kids' attention at the beginning of a class or activity. If you can grab them at the beginning, you'll have their attention for the rest of the time you are with them—but it's difficult to bring kids back once you've allowed their attention to wander.

Getting Attention
The first rule of thumb is to be confident and enthusiastic. A while ago there was a television commercial for an antiperspirant that said, "Never let them see you sweat," and this is doubly true when leading a group of children. Even if inside you're terrified at the prospect of leading, *never* let them know. If you're not confident you can engage kids' attention with an activity, don't do it. And if you're not interested in doing the activity, why would you expect the kids in your group to be?

In order to be confident, you need to know what you're going to do and say beforehand. You don't need to memorize a script, but you do need to have an outline in your head or written down on a piece of paper. It's good to practice out loud ahead of time, especially if you are telling a Bible story—you'll be more expressive and you'll have more confidence in your ability to captivate them with the story. In whatever activity you're leading, always speak clearly, slowly and authoritatively.

HAVE CONFIDENCE AND BE ENTHUSIASTIC!

One Sunday morning when I was leading a group of sixth-graders, another volunteer was introducing the activity that she'd chosen to help kids apply the Bible lesson to their lives. I never would have had the courage to do Ellen's activity with these sixth-graders! As she explained the activity, they made the typical "This sounds boring" grumbles that preadolescents are famous for, but Ellen continued to speak enthusiastically and lay out the supplies. She never let their comments get to her and she had confidence in the activity. To my surprise, soon the kids were happily engaged in doing

GAME HINT: After you explain the rules of a game, kids will have a multitude of questions. The more of these you answer, the less time you'll have for actually playing the game and the quicker you'll lose the attention of the whole group. To avoid this painful Death by Inquiry, anticipate some of the questions when you're first explaining the game and then tell the group that you'll deal with questions as they come up while the game is being played. If you're leading a large group, it's helpful for small-group leaders and teachers in the room to know a little about the activity ahead of time (or at least pay really good attention while you're explaining it!) so that they can answer questions from their own groups.

and learning. Ellen's success taught me a big lesson about the importance of confidence and enthusiasm to get kids' attention.

Anytime you introduce something to kids with a visual—particularly a DVD clip—you'll grab their attention. This generation of kids is the ultimate technology generation, so anytime you can use tools like a movie, video game or a television show, you'll grab their curiosity and their attention. (Just be careful not to overuse them—because then you'll be predictable!)

Attention-getters involving some kind of game will engage kids every time. Even if you share a classroom with other groups or have a small space for your activities, you can still use games—they don't all have to be active and noisy. Just make sure the game relates in some way to the topic you'll be teaching and discussing.

Depending on the age group you're working with, a provocative question, open-ended scenario or role play can grab their attention as they talk about what they'd do if they were in that particular situation. For example, you might teach the story of the Good Samaritan by asking the kids to suggest different endings than the one Jesus offered. Encourage them to act out those endings, then talk about why Jesus chose the ending to the story that He did.

Keeping Attention

Keep things moving. Anytime you leave the front of the group or pause in what you're saying because you left an important prop or supply in the back of the room (or worse, in your car!), you will lose the kids. They will find another activity to occupy their time, and it will probably not be the activity you desire them to be involved in. Make sure you have all your supplies at hand—it's important to keep things moving so that you can hold their interest.

Sometimes it helps to use a certain kind of signal as an attention-focuser. When kids hear or see this signal, they know it's time for them to quiet down and give you their attention. Flash the lights, use some kind of noisemaker, clap your hands or ask kids to put their hands in the air. This signals to them that the activity is about to begin or that behavior needs to be brought back under control. Tell the kids what kind of behavior you expect from them and why. Kids don't always know what is expected of them, so spell it out and go over it each week if they don't seem to get it.

If you're leading an activity for a large group, always enlist the help of the other volunteers or leaders in the room. Small-group leaders or shepherds should be sitting with their group, ready to help them pay attention—they should not be drinking coffee and chatting with the other volunteers in the back of the meeting space!

HOW DO I KEEP MY GROUP FROM GETTING OUT OF CONTROL?

Clearly define your behavioral expectations and remind the kids often. Everywhere kids go there are different expectations, and it's important that you establish yours so that they don't get confused. Kids can't be expected to follow rules that they don't know about!

It's important to keep rules simple so that kids can remember them. Once I did a teacher training workshop in a church located in the community where I lived. On the wall of the classroom was a floor-to-ceiling list of rules for the kids to follow. I pitied the children in that church—who could remember all those rules?

Here are my three behavioral expectations:

1. When I'm talking or another adult is talking, the group listens without talking.

2. When another kid in the group is talking, everyone else shows respect and listens to what she has to say.

3. "What's yours is yours." This means that everyone is expected to keep his hands to himself and no one can touch something

that belongs to someone else without first asking permission.

As the group leader, you need to decide for yourself what "out of control" means. Some adult leaders have more tolerance for boisterous children and their activities than others, as well as more confidence about their ability to gain back any lost control. You need to figure out when your group is verging on "out of control" and pull them back to a semblance of "in control" again. (Kids *will* need to be pulled back. They don't have disciplined mechanisms—like adults—to reign themselves in when things get a little too loud and crazy.)

I know I've said this many times already, but it bears repeating: Preparation is the best insurance against out-of-control kids. When you're prepared, you can move them seamlessly from one activity or discussion after another. When you're prepared, you have all your supplies at your fingertips and don't need to shift your attention away from the kids in order to rummage in your supply box or closet. When you're prepared, you can anticipate which activities have the most potential to get kids wound up and you can plan a defusing strategy in advance.

For example, I remember looking at a published curriculum that suggested the teacher decorate the room for a party. The learning activity involved telling the kids that the party had been cancelled and that they had to "undecorate" the room immediately. I remember imagining how the fifth- and sixth-graders I worked with would respond to that: I had a mental picture of them running wildly around the room, ripping down crepe paper and popping balloons. Needless to say, I didn't use that particular activity with those kids!

> # PREPARATION IS THE BEST INSURANCE AGAINST OUT-OF-CONTROL KIDS.

If you have a group that seems to always be out of control, you probably have more than you can handle. It's time to go to your supervisor/director or your children's pastor and ask for advice. You deserve a good experience at church with these kids as much as they deserve one with you.

HOW CAN I MANAGE MY GROUP OF OLDER KIDS?

Sometimes managing older grade-school kids presents more of a challenge than handling younger children. They are physically bigger and are more apt to push behavioral boundaries because of their higher level of reasoning ability. It is best to be proactive rather than reactive when it comes to discipline and classroom management.

First, make sure the group is clear about what is expected of them. Kids are in lots of different groups and each one has different behavioral expectations. Spell yours out, and often. Also, it's important if you team-teach for both of you to have the same rules and the same level of enforcement. If you don't, the kids will be confused and each of you will have a harder time managing the behavior of the group.

Don't be afraid to move kids around. Sitting next to one's friend is a privilege, not a right. If you have two kids who can't sit next to each other without being disruptive, move them away from each other.

Spotlight positive behavior and ignore negative behavior as much as you can. Often negative behavior is simply a plea for attention from you or the rest of the group. When we pay attention to a child for negative behavior, we're giving her exactly what she wanted and reinforcing the notion that negative behavior is the way to be noticed. If instead you develop a pattern of pointing out when kids are doing what you asked—and there's always at least one kid who strives to please you—this notice may prod the others to seek positive rather than negative attention. Of course, there will be actions you can't ignore—but consider carefully what these might be and plan for them in advance.

Never set a consequence that you can't enforce. If you tell a child he will lose five minutes of game time if he does a certain behavior again, make sure he loses five minutes of game time. If you do not, you'll lose all credibility with the group and they will never believe that you will enforce the consequences. Also, don't give a child what he wants as a consequence of negative behavior. For example, if a child is acting out because he doesn't want to participate in a certain activity, removing him from the activity as a consequence of his behavior will only give him what he's seeking and reinforce the negative behavior.

Sometimes with older kids, it's better to set incentives for positive behavior rather than consequences for negative behavior. You can establish a series of rewards for individuals or the whole group when the rules are followed. Some teachers have a special jar or box where a slip of paper with the child's name goes every time a kid does what is asked of her. At the end of the quarter, those kids with the most slips of paper gain a special reward. Conversely, names can be removed from the jar or box as a consequence of inappropriate behavior.

NEVER SET A CONSEQUENCE THAT YOU CAN'T ENFORCE.

Let me end this answer with a story. Once I worked with a small group of fifth- and sixth-grade boys, and they were some of the most rambunctious kids I'd ever met—they were so rowdy that I was reluctant to give the group to a volunteer and I took them myself.

One Wednesday evening I attempted to lead them in a short Bible study, but they weren't having it—disruption was everywhere. I was determined that this group was not going to get the best of me, so I informed them that I had no plans for the rest of the evening, and that we were going to make it through this Bible study even if it meant we had to stay beyond the program time.

One young man said that he couldn't stay longer because his mother drove by the curb to pick him up and he needed to be there at the right time or she wouldn't know where he was. "Well," I said to him, "I guess your mother won't be happy when you're not out there and she has to park the car and come into this very big building to look for you. And I bet she'll be even less happy when she finally finds you and discovers the reason you were late was your behavior here this evening."

They settled down and we successfully made it through the Bible story. They knew I would do what I said I would do.

WHAT DO I DO WITH A KID WHO JUST WON'T GET WITH THE PROGRAM?

How you deal with this child depends on how disruptive her actions are to the rest of the group. If her actions don't seem to affect the group's attitude toward you or the activity, you may want to just leave her alone.

Invite her into the group activity periodically and talk with her privately about why she is reluctant to participate. Observe her carefully from week to week to see what kinds of activities she enjoys and try to plan more of those (if possible). If you share your volunteer responsibilities with another person, talk with him about the child's participation when he is leading. Together you may figure a way to help her feel more a part of the group and the program.

If a child's actions are disruptive to the rest of the group, you need to take some action—one child should never be allowed to spoil the experience for the rest of the children. If he absolutely refuses to participate, ask him to sit quietly while the rest of the group is involved in the activity. Speaking with him privately can help, too. Find out what kinds of activities he is interested in and talk with him about how those activities might be incorporated in your program. Sometimes the child's actions are simply a plea for your attention or the attention of the other children. If you can find ways to give him positive attention, the problem might just go away.

If none of these ideas work, get some expert advice. Go to the person in charge of your program or your children's pastor and let her know what is happening. Chat with the child's parents if possible. Tell them you're concerned that their child isn't enjoying the program as much as the other kids and ask if they have any idea why that might be. Always try to partner with the parents of the children you work with.

Last, you may want to evaluate the activities you're offering the kids and how you're presenting them. Are they age appropriate? Are they frustrating to the children? Are they challenging to the children? Are you presenting the activities with enthusiasm? Observe how the whole group responds to the activities. It may be that you need to upgrade the teaching/learning methods you're using with your group.

WHAT CAN I DO TO HELP KIDS WITH ADHD FOCUS ON OUR ACTIVITIES?

ADHD is a condition characterized by problems with attention, impulsivity and over-activity. The child has trouble focusing on a project or activity, has problems sitting still, or continually does things without thinking about the consequences. While most children with this condition don't have all three of these characteristics, any one of them can be a challenge for a children's ministry volunteer! It's estimated that about 8 percent of children show symptoms of ADHD, so it's reasonable to expect that at least one child in your group will have this condition.

The American Academy of Pediatrics has offered some tips for teachers dealing with children with ADHD:

- If the child is able to read, display your classroom rules and behavioral expectations in a prominent place. Make sure your rules are clear and concise.

- Always provide clear directions for any activity and if the instructions are complex, divide them into smaller parts.

- If the child is easily distractible, sit him away from distractions and next to children who will be positive role models for staying on task.

- Provide a quiet place near your group meeting space where the child might work on a project alone.

- Remember that these children do better in small groups than large groups.

- Create a secret signal just between you and the child to use as a reminder when she is off task.

- Assist children with activity transitions. Provide clear directions and clues about finishing up a task or project. You might want to give a five minute warning to your group prior to any kind of transition to a new activity.

- Offer the child more positive reinforcement than negative consequences for behavior. Try to catch the child paying attention or on task and reward the child for that type of behavior.

- Specifically explain to the child what he needs to do in order to avoid negative behavioral consequences.[1]

It's been my experience that most parents are quite upfront with church volunteers about their child's ADHD. They will share with you what works best for keeping their child under control and on task and whether or not she is on any medication. However, there are still some parents who do not want other people to know their child has this condition.

If you suspect a child in your group might have ADHD, go to the supervisor/director of your program or your children's pastor and talk with him about it. He may be able to shed some light on the child and the family. If you decide that you need to chat with the parents about the kid's behavior in your group, don't diagnose the child for the parents. Instead, talk with them about the problems the child is having in your group and ask for their help. Ask for suggestions based on what they do at home or what the child's teachers do at school. Emphasize that your main objective is to provide a meaningful church experience for their kid, and that you truly care about the wellbeing of their child.

Note

1. Eileen Bailey, "ADD/ADHD in the Classroom—Ideas for Teachers." http://backtoschool.about.com/od/educatorscorner/a/tipsforteachers.htm (accessed December 12, 2006).

CHAPTER 6

THE HOME CONNECTION

Every church program for children needs to work in partnership with parents and families, because you are *all* responsible for the spiritual formation of the church's kids. Even though parents may not be present when you're with the kids, they remain a vital part of the spiritual formation equation.

HOW CAN I HELP PARENTS CONNECT WITH WHAT KIDS ARE LEARNING?

The first thing you can do is to get to know the parents of the kids in your group. If you are in a small church, you may already know each parent, but if you are volunteering in a large church, it's impossible to know everyone—some extra effort may be needed. Here are some suggestions:

If you work with younger children, a good opportunity to meet at least one parent is when Mom or Dad comes to drop off or pick up their kid from your program. Warmly introduce yourself and work at pairing up the right parents with each child.

If you work with older children, the parents may not drop off or pick up their kids. If that is the case, give the parent a call to introduce yourself. If you haven't been given contact information for the kids in your group, ask the coordinator of your program.

Class-Related Questions

Help parents become familiar with what their kids are learning so that they can continue the discussions at home. Some churches develop what could be called "In the Car Questions"—questions the parents can ask on the way home that are specific to that day's lesson. These questions might be something like "What did Jesus tell His disciples to do and why?" or for younger children "How did you learn how to be kind from your Bible story today?" Or give the kids a question to ask their parents at home, and ask them to share the answer when they come back the next week. Sometimes kids are more excited about being "the asker" than being "the questioned."

If your program has a musical component, send home CDs of the music with your kids. When these get played at home or in the minivan, it helps kids and parents learn the music together.

Parent/Child Groups

Consider inviting parents to observe or participate in your program or small group, or invite them to come toward the end of your time, and ask the kids to explain to the parents what they are learning. (Remember to talk with your program coordinator first.) It's not a good idea to have them come all at once—invite a few at a time depending on class room and group size. A group of first-grade teachers in our program had the kids make invitations for their parents, and both parents and kids had a great time.

My most successful "parent training" activities are those where the parents and kids take the class together. This shared experience helps them make memories together and have a spiritual topic in common to talk about at home. (And it's a great way to train parents to talk about spiritual things with their kids without them even knowing they are being trained!) If I hold a parent training event entitled "How to Teach Your Children about Advent," hardly anyone will come; but if I invite parents and kids to come and learn about Advent together, I'll get a good crowd.

Most parents will attend events with their kids, especially if they think the activity is for their kids and not for them. Providing a space and opportunity for families to learn about God together is a great way to connect with the home and strengthen the faith community.

Open House

In the middle of the program year, invite parents for an open house. They can learn the songs the kids sing, play some of the games, and hear a Bible lesson. This helps them connect with what their kids are doing at church, and allows them to interact with you and other parents.

WHAT ARE SOME ACTIVITIES FOR THE WHOLE FAMILY?

Many churches provide great age-segregated programming but don't think about ways to bring families or generations together. Here are some ideas to bridge the age gap:

Service Projects and Mission Trips

In our pastoral staff meetings at a church where I served, the Missions and Outreach Pastor would talk about various mission trips and service projects he was planning, and I'd often have to remind him to "think family": service projects and missions trips that whole families could do together. Finding projects or trips that entire families can participate in may take a little extra work, but that work is worth it—nothing can compare to the closeness a family experiences when they work together to serve others.

> **NOTHING CAN COMPARE TO THE CLOSENESS A FAMILY EXPERIENCES WHEN THEY WORK TOGETHER TO SERVE OTHERS.**

Service projects are one-time events where families work together with a group of people or a community organization. For example, this past

Halloween, fifth- and sixth-graders and their families from my church went to a local children's agency to host a party for kids who were part of the tutoring program. When whole families participate in service projects, kids see their parents serving other people, and they have an opportunity to get to know other adults as they work together on the project.

Mission trips are longer events and families often travel somewhere to do the service over a few days. For example, in the winter of 2005, several families from my church were part of a large group that traveled to Biloxi, Mississippi, to help the victims of Hurricane Katrina. Mission trips give an opportunity for families to participate together in a different culture and allow them to live together in a context quite different from their usual daily lives. This can be a great impetus for discussion of what it means to live as people who follow Jesus.

Church Business

Many times church business meetings are seen as "adults only" events and children are shuttled off to watch a video or play games, but I believe it is important for kids to see how a community of faith grapples with the issues and concerns of living together as the people of God. For our church's business meetings in the past, I set up activity tables in the back of the room with quiet activities like play dough and coloring pages. The kids were able to play at the tables and wander back to their parents when they needed some parental attention. (The biggest problem I had was keeping the adults away from the tables—they wanted to play, too!)

Combined Classes

I have seen some churches that have small groups for families, in which parents and kids participate in Bible study together. In this setting, kids see their parents talk about what a certain Bible story or passage means to them, as well as talk about and demonstrate God's values. Again, this takes more work than a small group that is just for adults, and the group may not want to do it long term, but it can be a powerful experience for families to study together for a few months or in the summer.

Think about having an intergenerational learning group that is open to everyone—singles, teens, empty nesters, older adults—not just families with kids. These classes provide opportunities for the generations to learn from each other and for kids to form relationships with adults they might not ordinarily have a chance to talk with. These classes take extra effort to find curriculum that works for all age groups and to convince people without children that they should come. I know from my experience with intergenerational learning groups, however, that they're worth the effort.

At one church where I served, our entire Sunday School—grade-school children through adults—combined in one intergenerational class every summer. During one session, each group (made up of both children and adults) had to create a skit from a Bible story and perform it for the rest of the class. The results were hilarious and the activity helped adults and children learn to work together and listen to each other—and everyone involved looked at the Bible stories in new ways.

HOW CAN I MEET THE NEEDS OF KIDS WHO COME TO CHURCH WITHOUT PARENTS?

Whenever I talk or write about the family as the center of spiritual formation for children, I always hear this question in the back of my mind: What about those kids whose parents have no interest in being part of the faith community? How do we spiritually nurture them?

There really isn't a good answer for this question, because without familial support, children miss a crucial element in the care of their soul. However, this lack of spiritual encouragement is where the church—the community of faith—can step in to become a surrogate family.

By being a teacher or small-group leader, you are in a great position to influence a kid's spiritual development by loving him, getting to know him, and caring about what is going on in his life. The relationship that you establish with a child becomes even more important to his spiritual development when it's not supported at home.

Recruit other families to adopt these children when they are at church programs. If you have children come to part of the community's worship service, kids whose parents don't attend could sit with their adopted families, or if your church serves a meal before your midweek program, these kids could eat with their adopted families. The church could also support the kids by purchasing the meal for them.

Always invite non-attending parents to the same events as church parents. Make sure you have their contact information. They just might surprise you some day and show up, and when they do, be prepared for them! Welcome them into the group and make sure that other parents talk with them rather than just chatting with people they know. If they feel included and accepted even one time, it is likely they will return for more.

Follow up on any kid whose parents don't attend if she misses even one meeting, class or event. She may not have a lot of control over when she can come to your church programs, so make sure you contact her and let her know she's been missed. Ask if there is anything you can do, such as give her a

THE COMMUNITY
OF FAITH
CAN STEP IN TO
BECOME A
SURROGATE FAMILY.

ride to and from church. This lets her and her family know that the people at church care about her, which can be a powerful draw to people who are unchurched.

If a church family has brought a neighbor kid to church, talk with them to find out a little bit more about the kid's family. If the church family has a friendship established with their neighbors, they will have an opportunity to invite the whole family to church or to a special church program. These church families can also be frontline friends in the spiritual nurture of these kids.

HOW CAN I HELP KIDS WHO ARE IN A DIFFICULT FAMILY SITUATION?

Some parents—even church parents—find themselves in such a difficult situation that they cannot even begin to think about the soul care of their children. This is a time when the church community must band together to help the children by nurturing them spiritually and helping them deal with their family difficulties.

Often we may not know the struggles families are facing—some people would rather go it alone than tell others about their problems, or sometimes confidentiality issues come into play. But there are some signs that indicate when a child is in a difficult family situation:

- If a child is usually regular in attendance and suddenly becomes irregular or consistently absent

- If a child usually enjoys being at church and suddenly has difficulty joining activities or

- If a child is generally well-behaved and suddenly begins to act out with inappropriate behavior

If you have a child in your group who you suspect is facing serious issues at home, consult the coordinator of your program or the children's pastor. She may be able to shed some light on the situation, without crossing any confidentiality boundaries, and offer you some advice on how to help this child.

Once you're aware of a child with a difficult family situation, it's important to make that child's church experience as positive as possible so that he views church as a safe place, a place where he can expect the unconditional love and forgiveness he may not be getting in his family.

Work hard to provide consistency for the child. If you job-share with another volunteer, make sure the child knows when to expect you and the other volunteer. He needs to know that he can depend on you both.

Make sure the child understands the behavioral expectations and be consistent with them. Again, this child may be acting out because of his home situation, and it's important to enforce your rules with love, understanding and consistency.

Let the child know you are available if he needs to talk with someone. Be aware, though, that occasionally when a child who is dealing with family dysfunction feels secure with a person, more acting-out behavior can result. This is because the child feels safe to express his negative feelings.

WHAT SHOULD I DO IF I SUSPECT A KID IS BEING ABUSED?

There are several reasons your suspicions might be aroused that a child is being abused:

- If a child shows signs of physical mistreatment—bruises, scratches, burns—that don't resemble the usual rough-and-tumble scrapes kids get themselves into just by being kids

- If a child becomes withdrawn or shows a drastic change in behavior

- If the child alludes to abuse or tells you outright that he's been abused

In any case, *never* take a situation like this into your own hands. Tell your supervisor/director or children's pastor your suspicions. Most states have what is called a "mandatory reporting law"—which means that people in certain occupations, such as teachers and ministers, are required by law to report any suspected abuse to the authorities—so be aware that when you talk with someone, they may be required by law to report it. This should never stop you from disclosing what you suspect, but it should make you carefully consider what you think you see.

Be very careful about jumping to conclusions. Once a suspicion is reported to law enforcement, various agencies will investigate and the family will be thrown into a difficult situation. Investigation is a good and necessary thing if abuse *is* happening, but it is a nightmare for a family if it is *not* happening, as they try to defend themselves against those who have an assumption of guilt.

No one wants to be responsible for leaving a child in an abusive situation, but it's important to be as sure as is reasonable about your suspicions before moving forward. Watch the situation for a few weeks to see if more than one of the indicators mentioned above appear to be present in the child's situation. Listen carefully to the child. Don't ask her specifically if she is being abused, but let her know that she can talk with you if she desires. This is another good reason to know the families of the children in your group. Relationship makes it easier not to jump to erroneous conclusions in an area as important and serious as abuse of a child.

CHAPTER 7

THE RED TAPE

Just like any other organization, most churches have systems and processes that are in place to ensure quality and consistency and to promote improvement. These procedures may include background checks, yearly evaluations and standards for conduct and behavior, and while they may seem like unnecessary hoops for jumping through, they are in place for the protection of both children and volunteers.

WHAT'S THE DEAL WITH BACKGROUND CHECKS?

It is an unfortunate but true sign of the times that churches must submit their volunteers to background checks. Churches cannot afford to allow adults to work with minors without knowing about past indiscretions. Not only does your church want to avoid being embroiled in a lawsuit, but it also wants to provide the safest environment possible for children who attend the church's programs. The background check is also for your protection, in the unlikely case that you are ever accused of inappropriate actions with a child. You can point to your spotless background check as a way to maintain your innocence.

Sometimes churches think they don't need to do background checks for their volunteers because "we know everybody" or "they've been in the church for years." But the truth is, we never know everybody, even when they have attended the church for years. There have been too many examples in both large and small churches of long-time church members acting inappropriately with children for any church to think that it can be exempt from checking out its volunteers—but please don't let this process get in the way of volunteering with the kids at your church.

> **YOUR CHURCH WANTS TO PROVIDE THE SAFEST ENVIRONMENT POSSIBLE FOR CHILDREN.**

You will most likely be asked to submit your Social Security number, because this is the way most agencies trace past arrests or convictions. In these days of identity theft, you are right to be concerned about who will have access to this information. Find out from the supervisor/director where the forms you submit are stored and who might be given access to your personal information. (Hopefully the information is kept in a locked file to which only the church administrator or another pastor has access.) While it's important for you to submit to the background check, it's also important for the church to keep your personal information safe.

You are well within your rights to ask exactly what parts of your background are being checked. Most churches look for past arrests or convictions for abuse charges with minors. Some churches may also check driving records if there is a chance the volunteer will be driving kids to and from activities. However, there is no reason to check your financial background, and you should be informed and give your consent if they intend to do so.

If you have any kind of adult criminal record, I encourage you to go to a leader at your church and talk to her about it. Let the church leadership decide what to do. If your record has been clean for a while and you are an upright citizen, there probably won't be a problem with your ability to volunteer in the children's ministry. (If you are unwilling to disclose that information, you should consider volunteering in another area of your church's ministry.)

If you have ever been arrested for any kind of child endangerment or abuse, however, you will be disqualified from working with children and youth. Even though you may have cleaned up your act and changed from those days in your past, no church can risk the potential legal repercussions of allowing you to work with minors. If this applies to you, find another place in your church to volunteer—there are plenty of ministry areas in your church that need you!

There is one more situation that might disqualify you from working with children, and it won't show up on a background check. If you were sexually abused as a child or teenager, some churches will not allow you to volunteer with children. The reason for this is the tendency for the abused to become abusers themselves. This may seem unfair to you—especially if you've never entertained thoughts of sexually abusing children—but some courts have found churches liable for negligence because they allowed someone who was abused to work with children, and they ended up abusing those in their care.

Many churches ask about childhood abuse on their volunteer applications, and it is in your best interest and the best interest of the church to answer truthfully, as painful as it may be. You should also request to talk with your pastor or children's pastor privately about the matter. There are some church policies that say such situations will be determined case by case, and you may be able to volunteer on a limited basis.

The bottom line is that it is extremely important to tell the truth, even if you might be embarrassed or find it painful. It is also vital that the leadership of your church shows discretion in how they use your personal information. You need to be assured that this information is kept confidential and only given to people who really need to know.

NOTHING IS MORE
DAMAGING TO A CHILD'S
SPIRITUAL FORMATION
THAN BEING HARMED
BY SOMEONE WHO
IS SUPPOSED TO
PROTECT THEM.

WHAT'S THE STORY BEHIND STANDARDS OF CONDUCT FOR VOLUNTEERS?

You must follow your church's every policy regarding volunteer behavior with children and youth. They haven't put these policies into practice to make your job more difficult, but to protect the children, the church and you.

In my experience, it's the policies that stipulate the kind of touch appropriate between an adult volunteer and a child, and those that set down what a volunteer can and can't do with a child outside of scheduled church activities, that meet the most resistance. Your church policies might tell you that you may only touch a child from the shoulders up, or that you must ask the child's permission before you hug her or put her on your lap.

From your perspective it may seem that your church is overdoing it, but that's not the case. It's very easy for children to misunderstand things, especially children who have been taught from a very young age to resist the touch of someone they don't know well. For many kids, "stranger danger" has been drilled into them from the time they were toddlers, and it's quite possible that an innocent, affectionate touch could be misunderstood. That child then goes home and tells his parent what happened at church, and suddenly you're accused of inappropriately touching a minor, and all this because of a misunderstanding.

This is also the reason your church policy probably states that you should never be alone in a room with a child—that there should always be at least two adults present. You always want a witness in the event that something you do is misunderstood by a child. I tell volunteers who help young children in and out of the bathroom never to go into the stall with a child, and if a child requests help to button or zip her pants, to take her into the hall or the classroom so that you can assist her with others present. This way nothing can be misunderstood.

Sometimes children's ministry volunteers desire to do things with church kids outside of regularly scheduled activities. Before you arrange an outside event, check your church's policy. Some churches prohibit outside activities, others have very strict rules about what is and isn't acceptable, and others allow these kinds of events but only on the church campus. Again, it's very important for you to follow your church's policy on these matters. The rules have been put in place for the protection of you and of the children. (I know I'm repeating myself, but I don't think I can say it enough!)

Whenever I have to set policies that restrict what ministry volunteers can do with kids, I feel very sad that we live in the kind of world where faith communities have to be so cautious. But this is reality, and without good guidelines, it's easy for those who wish harm to have access to our children, and we must guard these precious ones to nurture their faith. Nothing is more damaging to a child's spiritual formation than being harmed by someone who is supposed to protect them.

Always follow your church's volunteer behavior policies. If you need clarification about something, talk to your children's pastor or program coordinator.

WHAT SHOULD I DO IF I AM ACCUSED OF INAPPROPRIATE BEHAVIOR?

Take it very seriously. Some people find such accusations so absurd that they can't believe others will take them seriously. But they will: Law enforcement, social services, prosecutors, therapists and parents all take accusations of inappropriate behavior with a minor very, *very* seriously. Immediately seek legal advice. Don't try to handle it yourself.

You may not be able to depend on your church to help you. While the church will not be criminally liable, there is still a possibility that the family of the child may file a civil suit and sue the church for negligent hiring and supervision. The church will probably be advised by their attorney to remove you from your volunteer position and remove itself from any aspect of your defense. They might even ask you to stop attending church for the duration of the investigation and/or trial.

This is something you never want to have happen to you, and that's why you must never allow yourself to be alone with a child. Everything you do with children in your volunteer position should be done in full view of other people. Always protect yourself as well as the children.

HOW CAN I EVALUATE MY VOLUNTEER EXPERIENCE?

Here is a list of questions that will help you evaluate your volunteer experience and figure out where you should go from here:

1. *Did the volunteer experience meet your goals and expectations?* Everyone has reasons for volunteering as well as expectations for what the experience will be like. Think about how the experience measured up to yours. Did you hope to build relationships with kids in your church? If so, how well did that happen? Did you hope to work with your own kids and learn something about how to nurture them spiritually? If so, did that happen for you? Did you hope to use your gift of teach-

ing or leadership in a ministry at your church? If so, were you able to do that?

2. *Did you have time and energy to fulfill your responsibilities well?* Were you able to prepare for your duties and attend consistently, or did other demands get in the way of your commitment? Did fulfilling your responsibilities stress you out?

3. *Did you enjoy the experience? Did you look forward to being there most of the time?* Did you enjoy the age level of kids you worked with? What was it like working with the other volunteers?

I mostly enjoyed my experience, but . . .

Just because you answered "no" to some of these questions doesn't mean you shouldn't volunteer next year—it may just mean you need to make some changes in your commitment. If the experience didn't fulfill your expectations, talk with your supervisor/director or children's pastor about finding a place to volunteer that would better meet those expectations. If you found yourself unable to satisfy the volunteer commitment, perhaps you need a different kind of volunteer job in the children's ministry. Maybe you need to work with a different age level in order to enjoy it more. (For example, if you enjoy having deep conversations with kids, you'll be more excited about working with pre-teens than with preschoolers.)

Volunteering with children is the most important job anyone can do (yes, I'm a little biased) and people like you are in short supply, so please weigh your commitment, asking God to guide you in your decision.

> # VOLUNTEERING WITH CHILDREN IS THE MOST IMPORTANT JOB ANYONE CAN DO.

I didn't enjoy my experience

Figure out what you didn't like about volunteering with children in your church. Was there a part of the experience you found especially frustrating that could be changed? Perhaps you were not working with an age group of children you enjoy—you were given a rambunctious group of fifth-graders, when really you'd be more comfortable with the slower pace of three-year-olds.

Maybe you volunteered to work with your own child's group and that was a disaster. Now you know it's best not to be with your own children and you might try another position away from your kids.

Perhaps you volunteered for a job for which you're not well-suited. Maybe you volunteered for a coordinating position that requires you to deal with a lot of details, but you know you are not really an administrator and you've been frustrated all year. Ask for a job you will enjoy! Do you like to tell stories? Do you like to play with kids and help them do projects and other activities? People who feel competent in a volunteer position they enjoy are more likely to feel fulfilled by their experience.

Maybe you didn't get along well with the other volunteers. You were hoping to work as a collaborative team, and instead everyone just did their own thing. Or the volunteers you worked with were cliquey. (Yes, this happens in churches.) You felt left out and ignored by people who had worked together a long time. If this was the case, talk with your program coordinator or children's pastor before you give up. Let her know what happened to you. Perhaps she can find people with whom you'd enjoy working.

Or maybe you are just one of those people—and they do exist—who just aren't gifted to be with groups of children. That's okay! While you might enjoy your own kids or other children one or two at a time, you just feel overwhelmed by 5 or 6 or 10 kids at once. If that's the case, it's certainly okay not to volunteer again. I commend you for giving it a go—lots of people just assume they are not suited for it without even trying.

If, after you've examined all your reasons for not enjoying your volunteer experience, you feel there is nothing that could be done to help you feel happy and fulfilled working with children, of course it's alright not to return to your position. But please find some other area to volunteer in your church. Every ministry needs willing and committed people!

I need to take a break

It's absolutely fine for people who have worked with children for years to take a sabbatical. (A *sabbatical* is a year for rejuvenation after many years of teaching.) A sabbatical allows you to "top off your tank" by attending an adult study class or cultivating new adult relationships. It helps you find a new perspective on the work you do with children in the church. You'll come back to teaching renewed and ready to take on new challenges!

I know so many teachers who don't do anything to help themselves grow spiritually, even skipping worship services because of their teaching commitment. No one can continue to be an effective volunteer with children without minding the care of his own soul. If you need to take a year off to tend your own spiritual formation, please do so.

It's difficult for those of us who recruit volunteers year after year to let a good one go for a sabbatical, because people like you are hard to come by! We are secretly afraid that you won't come back after your sabbatical is over. So . . . if you take a year off, please come back.

One thing you might do during your sabbatical year is offer to be a substitute for the children's ministry. You still keep your hand in what's going on, but you get to take some well-deserved time off.

I want to change jobs

When I invite volunteers to sign up for the next year, I never assume they'll want to continue doing the same job, and most people I know who manage volunteers in a children's ministry are just happy to have volunteers come back for another year. They are usually more than happy to move volunteers to another job or age group. Occasionally there is one ministry area that runs poorly because of a lack of volunteers, while another area has a line a mile long of people who want to be a part of it. This makes staffing a children's program very difficult. If you want to make a change, please plan to move to an area where you are really needed—your ministry coordinator will bless you!

If no one asks where you'd like to volunteer next year, go to the person in charge of your program. Explain that you'd like to continue volunteering with kids, but you'd like to make a change in your position. Ask what other kinds of volunteer positions are available, or tell this person the kind of thing you'd like to do as a volunteer.

Be willing to stay where you are until an agreeable change—for everyone—can be made. This willingness lets the person in charge know that you are serious about continuing to work with children. (But also be willing to remind them you are still waiting for a change in your area of ministry!)

Everyone benefits when volunteers work in a position where they feel confident and fulfilled.

CHILDREN'S MINISTRY WORK: A HIGH CALLING

I think that being a children's ministry volunteer is more important than being an elder or a deacon or a member of the Board of Trustees. There is no higher call in a church than to help children learn to love God and follow Jesus.

While working with kids may be the most important job in the church, it's definitely not the easiest. Kids are noisy, messy and sometimes just plain stubborn. Preparation time means added items on your already-crowded calendar. The rewards are not always immediate. You may feel that you have not had enough training or that you are inadequate. Some weeks you may leave your group wondering if you're accomplishing anything meaningful.

Trust me, you are.

You're accomplishing something meaningful when you make your church environment a warm, welcoming and safe place. You're accomplishing something meaningful when you are a consistent and trustworthy example of a follower of Jesus—you're helping kids understand that God is consistent and trustworthy, too. They may not remember the details of every Bible story you teach or all the Beatitudes word for word, but you're influencing them spiritually in ways you may never know.

I recently participated in my church's fifth- and sixth-grade youth program with some boys who are rowdy and rambunctious and often need to be reminded about boundaries of appropriate behavior. The project of the day was to make a Thanksgiving collage, and at the end of our time, we sat in a circle and shared our collages with each other.

One boy who is especially high-energy shared his collage, on which was a picture of a person he admired. Over the picture he'd drawn a cross. He explained that while he liked this person, he didn't always live the way he should. The cross represented the boy's hope that this person would come to know Jesus and change the way he lived.

I admit I was very surprised. After having watched this boy from afar over the previous few months, I never expected to find this kind of reflection and consideration—and I was quite moved by what he had to say. I was reminded again that we can never really know what God is or isn't doing in the life of a child. If you strive to be an effective children's ministry volunteer, God *will* use you in ways you might not think possible. Never be discouraged because you can't see the fruit of your labor. You plant the seed; God grows the fruit.

I hope you've found this book helpful. I hope you have found some inspiration to help you be a more confident volunteer. My prayer for you is that you love the children you work with and find yourself growing, thriving and totally fulfilled. I pray that God works through you to help children learn to love God and follow Jesus.

RELUCTANT VOLUNTEERS

WHY ARE SOME PEOPLE RELUCTANT TO VOLUNTEER FOR CHILDREN'S MINISTRY?

"I don't have enough time." Many people feel they are too busy to volunteer with children at their church. They feel they don't have enough time to do the preparation and build relationship with the kids. People live very busy lives these days and it may be that some people really don't have enough time— but for others, I believe, it is a question of where one puts one's priorities. I'd like to suggest that it is more important to volunteer with kids at church than some of the other things people make time for.

"I've done my time. It's someone else's turn." Many times you hear this from older people or empty-nesters. They worked in the children's ministry when their kids were young, so they feel that they've taken their turn, done their duty—and now it's up to younger parents to take over. What these folks don't understand is that children are spiritually formed best when they have the opportunity to be in relationship with people from all generations, inside and outside their own families. At one of the churches where I was on staff, I had an empty-nester couple who really understood this. They volunteered every year to work with children in order to model the importance of mentoring children to their peer group.

"I'm not a Bible scholar. I don't know enough about the Bible to teach kids." Often people are reluctant to volunteer in children's ministry because they think they will be expected to be the "Bible Answer Person." They are worried that their lack of Bible knowledge will be a deterrent to teaching children well. Let me tell you a little secret: Teaching kids the Bible is a great way to learn about the Bible. There is an old adage that says, "The teacher learns more than the students," and this holds true for teaching the Bible: If you want to learn it, start teaching.

Through many years of recruiting volunteers, I've heard lots of reasons why people don't think they can volunteer to work with children. The people I appreciate the most are those who may not think they have the skills and talents but are willing to give it a try anyway. Many times they discover that they absolutely love it, and occasionally they realize that they are really not suited to work with children on a regular basis—but I respect them for giving it a try and refusing to assume it's something they can't do.

I'M A PARENT. WHY SHOULD I VOLUNTEER IN THE CHILDREN'S MINISTRY?

If you are a parent, you may yourself be reluctant to volunteer in children's ministry. After all, you work with your own kids all day every day—why should you sign up for a children's ministry position?

First, realize that you don't need to volunteer to lead the class that your children attend. Some kids do really well with their parents in church program situations and others don't. If you don't want to volunteer with your child's age level, consider volunteering with kids just a little older than yours. This will help you as a parent to get a heads-up about what your child will be like in a few years.

Second, whether or not you volunteer with your children's class, recognize that volunteering gives you the opportunity to be involved in areas in which they are learning what it means to love God and follow Jesus. This will help you talk with your child at home about what she is learning and doing at the church programs. You'll have firsthand knowledge, whereas parents who don't help in the program don't always know how to talk with their kids about these spiritual topics.

Third, remember that volunteering will give you the opportunity to build relationships with other parents in your church. It will also enable you to meet people who don't have young children, which will enable you to build relationships with people who you might never connect with otherwise. You'll get to meet great kids and build your relationship with God as you help others build theirs.

Some parents enjoy working with children or enjoy teaching their own children at church, while others find it "just one more thing" added to their already too-busy lives. Don't feel you have to volunteer simply because you are a parent with children in the program. It may be that you have gifts and talents that are better used elsewhere. If you choose not to volunteer in the children's ministry, be available for other things the volunteers might ask of you, such as providing snacks for a programs or acting as "crowd control" for a special event. This shows that you realize how you need to give something back to those who give so much to your children.

Raise Your Children to Love Jesus

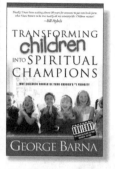

Transforming Children Into Spiritual Champions
Why Children Should Be Your Church's #1 Priority
George Barna
ISBN 08307.32934

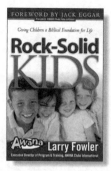

Rock-Solid Kids
Giving Children a Biblical Foundation for Life
Larry Fowler
ISBN 08307.37138

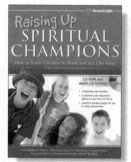

Raising Up Spiritual Champions
How to Teach Children to Think and Act Like Jesus
ISBN 08307.36638

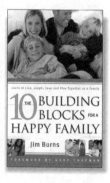

The 10 Building Blocks for a Happy Family
Learn to Live, Laugh, Love and Play Together as a Family
Jim Burns
ISBN 08307.33027

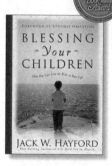

Blessing Your Children
How You Can Love the Kids in Your Life
Jack W. Hayford
ISBN 08307.30796
DVD • UPC 607135.008491

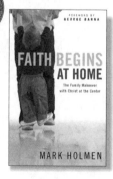

Faith Begins at Home
The Family Makeover with Christ at the Center
Mark Holmen
ISBN 08307.38134

Available at Bookstores Everywhere!

Visit **www.regalbooks.com** to join **Regal's FREE e-newsletter.**
You'll get useful **excerpts** from our newest releases and **special access to online chats** with your favorite authors. Sign up today!

Regal
God's Word for Your World™
www.regalbooks.com

HOW TO TEACH CHILDREN TO THINK AND ACT LIKE JESUS

"If people do not embrace Jesus Christ as their Savior before they reach their teenage years, the chance of their doing so at all is slim."

George Barna
Transforming Children into Spiritual Champions

Raising Up Spiritual Champions
How to Teach Children to Think and Act Like Jesus
A Discipleship Course for Ages 9 to 12

Help kids answer the big questions about what it means to think and act like Jesus every day of their lives! This eight-session discipleship program provides the tools teachers need—from meaningful discussion questions to creative activities, from student pages to parent pages—to nurture lifelong spiritual growth in their students. Because most children's spiritual beliefs are in place by age 13, it's crucial that they acquire a biblical foundation for how they view themselves and the world. This program will help leaders teach God's truth during these all-important preteen years!

ISBN 08307.36638
Reproducible Manual
with CD-ROM and Music CD

Raising Up Spiritual Champions Includes

- CD-ROM containing everything in this book, including awards, **Student and Parent Pages**, publicity flyers, customizable forms, clip art and more!
- 8 reproducible sessions with discussion questions and fun activities
- Reproducible music CD with 12 praise and session-related songs
- How-tos for setting up the program
- 12 teacher-training articles
- **Student Pages** for use in class and at home to build discipleship habits
- **Parent Pages** that support parents in their role of spiritual teachers
- Teaching resources, including skits, discussion cards, games and more!

To order, visit your local Christian bookstore or www.gospellight.com

Gospel Light
God's Word for a Kid's World!™
www.gospellight.com

SUNDAY SCHOOL
TEACHER
APPRECIATION DAY
Third Sunday in October

Honor Your
Sunday School Teachers

**On Sunday School Teacher Appreciation Day
the Third Sunday in October**

Churches across America are invited to set aside the third Sunday
in October as a day to honor Sunday School teachers for their
dedication, hard work and life-changing impact on their students.
That's why Gospel Light launched **Sunday School Teacher Appreciation
Day** in 1993, with the goal of honoring the 15 million Sunday School
teachers nationwide who dedicate themselves to teaching the
Word of God to children, youth and adults.

Visit **www.mysundayschoolteacher.com** to learn great ways to
honor your teachers on Sunday School Teacher Appreciation Day
and throughout the year.

NOMINATE YOUR TEACHERS
FOR SUNDAY SCHOOL TEACHER
OF THE YEAR!

**Winner Receives a Dream Vacation
to Hawaii!**

An integral part of Sunday School Teacher Appreciation Day is the
national search for the **Sunday School Teacher of the Year**.
This award was established in honor of Dr. Henrietta Mears—a famous
Christian educator who influenced the lives of such well-known and
respected Christian leaders as Dr. Billy Graham, Bill and Vonette Bright,
Dr. Richard Halverson, and many more.

You can honor your Sunday School teachers by nominating
them for this award. If one of your teachers is selected, he or she will
receive **a dream vacation for two to Hawaii,** plus free curriculum,
resources and more for your church!

Nominate your teachers online at **www.mysundayschoolteacher.com**.

Sponsored by

Gospel Light

*Helping you honor Sunday School teachers,
the unsung heroes of the faith.*

In Partnership With

259.22   117775

LINCOLN CHRISTIAN COLLEGE AND SEMINARY

B3978 U

3 4711 00180 1697